Restoring the Jewishness of the Gospel

Other products from JEWISH NEW TESTAMENT PUBLICATIONS, INC.

Messianic Jewish Manifesto
Jewish New Testament
Jewish New Testament Commentary
The Good News of Yeshua the Messiah,
    as Reported by Yochanan (John)
Jewish New Testament on cassette
Complete Jewish Bible

RESTORING THE JEWISHNESS OF THE G✡SPEL

A Message for Christians
Condensed from *Messianic Jewish Manifesto*

by

David H. Stern

JEWISH NEW TESTAMENT PUBLICATIONS, INC.
Post Office Box 615, Clarksville, MD 21029, USA

Stern, David H., 1935

    Restoring the Jewishness of the Gospel / by David H. Stern
— 1st ed. — Jerusalem, Israel: Jewish New Testament Publications, Inc.;
© 1988.

    85 p.: ill.; 21 cm.
    Includes bibliographical references and index.
    ISBN 965-359-0014 (pbk.)

    1. Jews in the New Testament.   2. Christianity and othe religions-Judaism.
3. Judaism—Relations—Christianity.   4. Missions to Jews.   I. Tide.

BS2545.J44S74   1988   225.6'7-dcl9   88-190144
                                          AACR 2 MARC

Library of Congress

Cover art by Elhanan Ben Avraham

Second edition (with revised Introduction, corrections and General Index)
Printed in U.S.A.

03   10 09 08

Published by
JEWISH NEW TESTAMENT PUBLICATIONS, INC.
Post Office Box 615, Clarksville, MD 21029, USA
410-764-6144

Distributed by
Messianic Jewish Resources International
a division of Lederer/Messianic Jewish Communications
6204 Park Heights Avenue, Baltimore, MD 21215-3600

Individual order line: 800-410-7367   Trade order line: 800-773-MJRI (6374)

E-mail: lederer@MessianicJewish.net   Website: www.MessianicJewish.net

CONTENTS

INTRODUCTION

"The truth, the whole truth, and nothing but the truth." The Gospel which the Church preaches, the Gospel of God's grace to individuals, expressed so perfectly in the first eight chapters of Romans and sometimes epitomized in four or five "spiritual laws," is the truth, and it is nothing but the truth. But it is not the whole truth. The whole truth requires restoring the Jewishness of the Gospel.

This book brings one simple message, namely, that unless the Church does everything in her power to restore that Jewishness, she lacks a key component of the Gospel. In consequence she cannot fulfill the Great Commission properly, and the Jewish people cannot be the right kind of "light to the nations." Rather than define what "Jewishness" means, I will let the whole book, in the process of presenting its message, convey the content and flavor of what it is that needs to be restored.

When the Church proclaims a Gospel without its Jewishness restored, she is at best failing to proclaim "the whole counsel of God" (Acts 20:27). At worst she may be communicating what Sha'ul [Paul] called "another Gospel" (Galatians 1:6-9). Moreover, not only Jews suffer from this off-target preaching — Gentiles suffer too. Therefore I believe I am focussing on an extremely serious problem which has not received from Christians the attention it deserves.

In speaking of restoring the Jewishness of the Gospel I assume that my readers will agree to the following three points,

1

which are not themselves part of this restored Jewishness but
are presupposed by it: (1) Christianity is Jewish, (2) antisemitism[1] is un-Christian, and (3) refusing or neglecting to
evangelize Jews is antisemitic. We will review these proposi-
tions in Chapter III, closing with an examination of what is
meant by the phrase in Romans 1:16, that the Gospel is the
power of salvation "to the Jew first."

The first two chapters present the main idea of the book.
Chapter I compares restoring the Jewishness of the Gospel with
the alternative of "contextualizing" it and concludes that the
latter is misdirected. Chapter II is the book's center of gravity,
a discussion of what gets changed when Jewishness is restored
to the Gospel.

Finally, Chapter IV surveys the blessings which will flow
from restoring the Jewishness of the Gospel. At the end is a
glossary of all Hebrew words and names used.

This little book is written primarily for non-Jewish Christians and for Jewish believers in Yeshua [Jesus] who have not
thought much about how Jewish their faith is. All the material
in it appears (with minor modifications) in a longer book,
Messianic Jewish Manifesto[2], whose primary intended reader-
ship is Jewish believers in Yeshua who identify positively with
their own Jewishness; others are encouraged to read it as if
looking over a Messianic Jew's shoulder. Therefore people who
wish to pursue further the ideas presented *in Restoring the*

---

1   In this book the word "antisemitic" is synonymous with "anti-Jewish." This
      usage is open to criticism on two counts. First, some Arabs may take offense
      because they too are Semites; but English-speakers do not mean "anti-Arab"
      when they say "antisemitic.' Second, I have heard a Christian object that the
      word 'antisemitism' too readily connotes the horrors of Hitler's Germany.
      While I am not trying to dredge up those memories every time the term
      appears, it must be recognized that antisemitism represents a spectrum not
      of good but of evil, from relatively minor sins to the worst imaginable.

2   David H. Stern, *Messianic Jewish Manifesto* (P.O. Box 615,Clarksville, MD
      21029, USA: Jewish New Testament Publications, Inc., 1988).

Jewishness of the Gospel, or who find that it raises more questions than it answers, or who wish to understand better my viewpoint on these matters ought to read *Manifesto.* Anyone who, after reading *Manifesto,* has questions, suggestions or criticisms is invited to communicate them.[3]

As for those, both Jewish and non-Jewish, who do not believe in Yeshua, it is not a purpose of the present book to convince them otherwise. There is no shortage of literature aimed at persuading people to believe in him. But this book assumes, without supplying proofs, that Yeshua is indeed Israel's Messiah, and that the New Testament and the *Tanakh* ("Old Testament") constitute God's word to humanity.

It has been pointed out to me that there are Christians who experience this book as promoting the Judaizing heresy which Sha'ul condemns in the book of Galatians. But "Judaizing" does not mean encouraging New Testament believers to investigate the Jewishness of their faith. Rather, it means one or a combination of the following three things: (1) insisting that Gentiles cannot be saved by faith in Yeshua the Messiah unless they convert to Judaism, (2) requiring saved Gentiles to follow Jewish cultural practices, and/or (3) legalism, i.e., requiring Gentiles to obey a perverted version of the Torah in which God's Law is seen as a set of rules unrelated to faith. Neither I nor the vast majority of Messianic Jews are Judaizers. I think that if this book is read in the light of what "Judaizing" really signifies, any fair reader should be convinced.

David H. Stern
December 1987 and May 1990

---

3   Communications may be sent to:

Dr. David H. Stern
P. O. Box 615
Clarksville, MD 21029, USA

CONTEXTUALIZATION VERSUS RESTORATION

A. Christianity And Culture.

1. "Transcultural Judaism."

Yeshua's "Great Commission" to the Church was to make disciples from every nation.[1] But as soon as the early Messianic Jews began reaching out to Gentiles, it was necessary to separate the Gospel from its cultural context, so that its essential message would not be encumbered with cultural baggage unnecessary for salvation.

Learning that the New Covenant did not require Gentiles to become Jews in order to be saved was a traumatic process for the Jewish believers in Yeshua [Jesus]. It began with Kefa's [Peter's] vision and Cornelius's coming to faith.[2] But it was Sha'ul [Paul], Yeshua's emissary [apostle] to the Gentiles, who worked out many of the details. Thus, he was present at the Jerusalem Council when Ya'akov [James] announced the decision that Gentiles would not have to get circumcised and obey the *Torah* [the Law] as it had developed within traditional Judaism. Instead, the only entrance requirement for them to be fully accepted as brothers in the Lord was obedience to the four *mitzvot* [commandments] outlined in Acts 15:20.

Later Sha'ul enunciated even more clearly the extent to which he was willing to go in order to win people — anyone,

---

1   Mattityahu [Matthew] 28:18-20.
2   Acts 10:1 — 11:18

Jewish or Gentile — to the Lord. He wrote, in 1 Corinthians 9:19-22:

> For although I am free from all men, I have enslaved myself to all, that I might win the more. To the Jews I became as a Jew, in order to win Jews; to those under law I became as one under law — though not being myself under law — in order to win those under law. To those apart from law I became as one apart from law — not being myself apart from law toward God but "en-lawed" to the Messiah — in order to win those apart from law. To the weak I became weak, in order to win the weak. I have become all things to all men, that I might by all means save some.

In quoting this text I am compelled, because of criticisms commonly made, to note that in becoming "all things to all men" Sha'ul was not presenting himself as a chameleon or a hypocrite. Rather, in saying he "became" like others he meant that he put himself in their position, empathized with them, tried to understand their mindset, paid attention to "where they were coming from" and "where they were at." What motivated him was his desire to win the lost. He could have been lazy, he could have demanded that others adapt themselves to his culture rather than he empathize with theirs. But God's call on his life constrained him to go the extra mile, indeed to "enslave" himself to the needs of others.

In sum, Sha'ul did not compel Gentiles to adopt Jewish culture. He realized that the New Testament message for Gentiles was really, in Phil Goble's words, "transcultural Judaism," or, as it has come to be known, Christianity.

2. Non-Transcultural Christianity.

But not everyone who has attempted to bring the Gospel message across cultural barriers has understood the principles of cross-cultural evangelism as Sha'ul taught them. Frequently the exact opposite happened: the Gospel was confused with culture, so that the message was not only to turn from sin to God through Yeshua, but also to abandon one's culture and become estranged from it.

In some parts of the world the missionaries lived (and still live) in a self-created ghetto, the "mission compound." When God touched a native and gave him a new spirit, the missionaries brought him into the compound and gave him a new culture (usually Western).

James Michener describes this approach graphically in his book, *Hawaii.* The book is historically inaccurate and filled with anti-Christian bias and prejudice, but we will adopt the author's perspective for a moment. He depicts missionaries from New England in the early 1800's requiring native Hawaiians to build wooden churches with steeples and dress like Puritans in order to become Christians. They had to become aliens in their own culture. True, the *kamaainas* often went about nude, and Christian discipleship entails modesty; nevertheless modesty does not necessarily entail adopting foreign dress. When people become Christians they need give up only their sin, not their culture, except the specific elements of it that violate Scriptural norms.

3. "Now That You're Christian, Have a Ham Sandwich!"

As far as Jewish evangelism is concerned, it became standard practice by the fourth century *not* to follow Sha'ul's pattern of presenting the Gospel in the way most congenial to those for whom it was intended. On the contrary, it was not enough that a Jew should accept Yeshua as his Messiah, Savior and Lord; he had to "convert to Christianity,"[3] which usually meant

---

3   As used here, "converting to Christianity" is meant to be contrasted with "becoming a Messianic Jew." Jewish converts to Christianity and Messianic Jews both believe in Yeshua, but the latter retain their Jewish identity (which means Jewish practices as well as Jewish thoughts) — precisely what Jewish believers from the fourth century

adopting an alien culture and sometimes required him to give up everything Jewish! The latter can be seen in this profession from the Church of Constantinople which Jews had to affirm if they wanted to join the holy Community of the Jewish Messiah, Yeshua:

'I renounce all customs, rites, legalisms, unleavened breads and sacrifices of lambs of the Hebrews, and all the other feasts of the Hebrews, sacrifices, prayers, aspersions, purifications, sanctifications and propitiations, and fasts, and new moons, and Sabbaths, and superstitions, and hymns and chants and observances and synagogues, and the food and drink of the Hebrews; in one word, I renounce absolutely everything Jewish, every law, rite and custom. ... and if afterwards I shall wish to deny and return to Jewish superstition, or shall be found eating with Jews, or feasting with them, or secretly conversing and condemning the Christian religion instead of openly confuting them and condemning their vain faith, then let the trembling of Cain and the leprosy of Gehazi cleave to me, as well as the legal punishments to which I acknowledge myself liable. And may I be anathema in the world to come, and may my soul be set down with Satan and the devils."[4]

---

onward were often forbidden to do. See below, Chapter II, Section B; and also my book, *Messianic Jewish Manifesto*, Chapter II. (In more recent times many Jewish converts to Christianity have voluntarily chosen to escape, ignore or limit their degree of Jewish identification.) Actually, in the New Testament the term "Christian" is not used by believers to refer to Messianic Jews but to Gentiles who came to know the one true God through Yeshua the Jewish Messiah. See *Manifesto*, Chapter II, Section C-4. Whether the term "Christian" should be applied to Messianic Jews today is discussed in *Manifesto*, Chapter III, Section H.

4   "Profession of Faith, from the Church of Constantinople: From Assemani, Cod. Lit., I, p. 105," as cited in James Parkes, *The Conflict of the Church and the Synagogue* (New York: Atheneum, 1974), pp. 397-398

More than once in recent times have Messianic Jews been required to "prove their Christianity" by eating a ham sandwich. I myself have on occasion experienced distinct uneasiness emanating from Christian leaders when they discover that my wife and I observe *kashrut* [the Jewish dietary laws].

B. Contextualizing The Gospel.

As modern-day missiologists — the scholars who help evangelists and missionaries in their work of obeying the Great Commission — began to look into the problem of people being removed from their culture in order to become Christians, they developed the concept of *contextualization*. The word simply means presenting the Gospel within the context of the recipient's culture, rather than outside it. One could even say it's just a fancy way of talking about what Sha'ul did naturally. When the Gospel is contextualized, new Christians remain within their culture and try to conform it as well as themselves to God's will.

1. Contextualizing The Gospel For Jews.

The founding of what came to be called the Hebrew Christian movement in England and other European countries during the nineteenth century was essentially an effort at contextualizing the Gospel for Jews. Jewish believers were advised not to leave their people but to stay Jewish, so long as their New Testament faith remained orthodox. They were encouraged to celebrate Passover, Chanukah and other festivals, and, generally, to express their Jewishness. They were also reminded that their observance of elements in the Mosaic Law did not enhance their salvation — like Gentiles they are saved by faith and not by "works of law."

Clearly contextualization was an improvement over requiring Jews to renounce everything Jewish. But it dealt with Jewish believers as problem individuals — rather than with Judaism and the Jewish people as a corporate entity standing

over against Christianity and the Church, and making conflicting claims concerning biblical truth.

2. Type I, Type II And Type III Evangelism.

Missiologists have come up with a threefold classification of the
cultural and linguistic barriers across which the Gospel must be
proclaimed.

Type I Evangelism is sharing with nominal Christians in one's
own culture. These are people who not only share one's
language and cultural background but may have grown up
going to church, hearing the Gospel and reading the Bible. In
short, they are "Christianized" but not born again. In terms of
ease of communication, this type of evangelism is the simplest.
(Whether it is easiest in terms of getting people saved is another
question.)

Type II Evangelism is with people who share one's language
and perhaps live in the same or a similar society, but whose
cultural and religious presuppositions may be very different.
Suburbanite white upper middle class Christians bringing the
Gospel to unsaved lower class blacks in the inner city — and
inner-city black Christians bringing the Gospel to unsaved
whites in the suburbs — are both engaged in Type II
Evangelism. So are Japanese Christians in Japan, where the
religious milieu is Buddhist and Shinto.

Type III Evangelism brings the Gospel across cultural and
linguistic barriers that at times can seem all but insuperable.
The idea is conveyed well by the traditional picture of the
missionary in a primitive jungle tribe learning the language,
inventing an alphabet, translating the Bible, fighting the alien
cultural and physical environment, all in order make God's
grace known. Likewise, the on-fire Christians of Korea or
Indonesia who preach to the blasé youth of Europe may find
themselves doing Type III Evangelism.

Each of these types requires its own approach to contextualization. To give one example, consider the verbal presentation of important theological concepts. In Type I Evangelism one can use "Christian language," with such terms as "sin," "born again" and "saved," the object being to deepen the hearer's spiritual understanding of what these mean, so that he will respond with faith. In Type II Evangelism such terminology seems peculiar and troublesome. These ideas must be conveyed differently to un-Christianized hearers, with examples from life, not jargon from church. In Type III Evangelism the language and culture may make it difficult to express the concepts at all.

3. Where Do The Jews Fit In?

Where do the Jews fit into this schema? If one regards Jewish people as candidates for Type II Evangelism, as un-Christianized members of the same society and language-group, then one is assuming that the Church is proclaiming the true Gospel, so that the task is only to contextualize it. Someone who takes this approach will argue that if a Samoan can be Christian and remain Samoan, why can't a Jew be Christian and stay Jewish?

Nevertheless, there is something strange, even wrong, in talking about contextualizing the Gospel for Jews; because the Gospel was completely Jewish in the first place! If Christianity's roots are Jewish, if the Gospel itself is Jewish in its very essence, why should it need to be contextualized for Jews?

The answer is that it doesn't need to be — provided the New Testament Gospel is actually being proclaimed! In fact, the Gospel had to be contextualized for Gentiles! That was Sha'ul's ministry. This was the victory of Acts 15, in which the Jerusalem Council decided that Gentiles did not have to become Jews in order to become Christians. This was the victory of Galatians 2, in which Sha'ul confronted Kefa [Peter] over Judaizing Gentile believers. The subsequent history leading to the outcome that *Jews* were required to be *Gentilized* in order to become Messianic shows how far practice strayed from the principles Sha'ul had set forth in the New Testament. It also signalled that something very strange had happened to the Jewish Gospel along the way!

And practice deviated not only from Sha'ul's principles, but from his practice as well. Sha'ul was a lifelong observant Jew. According to the Book of Acts, Sha'ul circumcised Timothy (Acts 16:3); regularly went to synagogue (17:2); took a Jewish vow (18:18); rushed up to Jerusalem to observe the Jewish pilgrim festival of *Shavu'ot* [Pentecost] (20:16); paid for other Jews to offer Jewish sacrifices at the Jewish Temple (21:23-27); stated before the Jewish Sanhedrin that he was then — as of that moment and not just formerly — a *Parush* [Pharisee] (23:7); and declared to the Roman governor, Festus, that he had "done nothing against the *Torah* to which the Jews hold, nor against the Temple" (25:8, *Jewish New Testament* version). Finally, having fought the good fight, finished the race and kept the faith, he could tell an audience of Jews in Rome, "I have done nothing contrary to the people or to the ancestral customs" (28:17) — the phrase "ancestral customs" including Jewish traditions and not only the Written *Torah*. If this kind of life was good enough for Sha'ul, it is good enough for Jewish believers today. No ham sandwiches, please, for Messianic Jews who keep *kosher*.

C. Not Contextualization But Type IV Evangelism.

Indeed any Jew can, like Sha'ul, be Messianic and remain Jewish. Nevertheless, to think this resolves all the issues is a great mistake because it misses the point. The reason is theological. From a sociological viewpoint, the Jews are just another culture, like the Samoans (actually it's not quite that simple, since there are many Jewish cultures).

But theologically, the Jews are unique because God chose them as the vehicle for bringing salvation to the world. The entire Hebrew Bible attests to that, as does the New Testament (see Yochanan [John] 4:22; Romans 3:2, 9:4-5). The Jews are God's people in a sense that applies to no other people on earth. Because of this, the New Testament abounds with theological Scyllas and Charybdises, rocky places that offer dangerous passage. What other people is faced with Galatians 3:28 ("there is neither Jew nor Greek") or Ephesians 2:11-22 ("the middle wall of partition")? If the French Christians Frenchify other believers, who raises any doctrinal question? But if Messianic Jews engage in Judaizing — watch out!

No, the Jewish people are more than a culture, they are the people of God. Therefore, the task in relation to Jews is not to contextualize the Gospel as it has come to non-Jews, with their pagan history, but rather to communicate a Gospel which is theologically correct vis-a-vis the Jewish people, whose history and role in communicating God's salvation is an eternal part of Holy Scripture. *Type IV Evangelism is needed to evangelize the people of God.*

To put it another way, contextualizing the Gentile form of the Gospel for the Jews is a double diversion. Originally its Jewish form was contextualized for Gentiles — this was Sha'ul's great contribution to evangelism. But then, as the early Messianic Jewish communities fell on hard times and disappeared, the Jewishness originally present in the Gospel also vanished, so that a Gentile-contextualized Gospel deprived of its Jewish substratum was the only Gospel there was, a Procrustean bed in which the Jewish believer was forced to lie. Recently this Gospel-at-one-remove (from a Jewish standpoint) has been reworked, contextualized, to make it "seem" more Jewish. But the double adaptation is not the same as the original. Looking at a person's mirror reflection reflected in a second mirror is not the same as looking at him.

What Type IV Evangelism requires is not a Gentilized Gospel contextualized for Jews, but a restoration of the Jewishness which is in fact present in the Gospel but which has become obscured. Moreover, Gentile Christians too need aspects of the Gospel which a restoration of its Jewishness will bring them.

But many believers feel uneasy about restoring Jewishness to the Gospel and encouraging Messianic Jews to express their Jewish identity. They fear an elitism will arise in which Gentile Christians will be made to feel like second-class citizens of the Kingdom. This is a real pitfall, and Scripture warns against division between Jew and Gentile in the Body of the Messiah. However, the New Testament also gives assurance that both are one in Yeshua, serving one God by one Spirit. Therefore, let all believers, both Jewish and Gentile, work together to avoid invidious comparisons, which only serve the Adversary. Let every Messianic Jew and every Gentile Christian demonstrate in his own life those elements of Jewishness which arise from his own spiritual consciousness and identity, without feeling condemned for expressing either too much or too little. And let each one remain open to God's leading, so that this aspect of his life, like all others, can be conformed more and more to the image of Yeshua, the Messiah of Jews and Gentiles alike.

Having warned against elitism and division, we ask what restoring the Jewishness of the Gospel actually entails. To this question we turn our attention now.

CHAPTER II

RESTORING THE JEWISHNESS OF THE GOSPEL

A. Definition.

Restoring the Jewishness of the Gospel means filling out the content of the Gospel in all its fullness as it pertains to Jews and to the relationship between the Jewish people and the Church. In other words, it means offering, in relation to these things, "the whole counsel of God," not just part.

It is important to understand what theologians mean when they talk about "restoration." We would all like to see the Church "restored" to what it was in the first century. Or so we say. Certainly it would be good to restore the zeal of the first believers, the righteousness of their lives, their willingness to follow Yeshua the Messiah no matter what the cost, their being filled with the Holy Spirit, their eagerness to pray, their assurance and experience that God performs miracles in response to faith. But are there external aspects of the first century believers' lifestyle that we should set out to restore? or aspects of doctrine that they would have accepted, but which later believers have ignored? And if so, which ones? and what should we do about them?

My view is that we ought to start by making every effort to *understand* the text of the New Testament as its first century hearers would have understood it and applied it to their situation in life. But I do not believe we are expected to apply the Gospel in the same way, because that would mean restoring the first-century situation in life, which, even were it desirable, is impossible — there is no turning back the clock. Rather, we must understand Scripture properly and then apply it to our own situation in the appropriate way.

The above paragraphs do not express a new philosophy. They express a familiar approach which normally leads to asking whether a given New Testament injunction is to be applied literally, or should one look for a general principle behind the written command. For example, in reference to 1 Corinthians 11:2-16, must a woman today cover her head in a congregation meeting? Or was this requirement related only to the first-century life situation, so that the modern application is to dress modestly by current standards?

I do not propose to enter into discussions of this kind at all. Rather, in bringing up the question of *restoring* the Jewish Gospel, I intend to call attention to aspects of the Gospel which would have been evident to first-century believers but which centuries of neglect have hidden from view.

B. The Church And Israel In Theology And History.

We start with three entities — Israel, the Jewish people and the Church — and we ask what are the relationships between them. We must examine the matter both theologically and historically. Theology will show us the true relationship, how things are "in the heavenlies," while history will show us what has happened here on earth. We will then be better able to consider what to do.

1. Three Theologies: Covenant, Dispensational And "Olive Tree."

Christian theologians have usually followed one of two approaches in dealing with this subject. The older and better known one is generally called Replacement theology or

Covenant theology, although it is also appearing these days under other names; it says that the Church is "Spiritual" Israel or the "New" Israel, having replaced the "Old" Israel (the Jews) as God's people. More recently there has developed in Protestant quarters Dispensational theology, which, in its more extreme form, says that the Jewish people have promises only on earth, while the Church has promises in heaven. We will not consider these approaches in detail, but the bottom line is that both oversimplify and in the process arrive at manifestly antisemitic[1] conclusions.[2]

The following analysis will show that the separation between the Church and the Jewish people, as it has developed over the last 2000 years, is completely out of God's will, a terrible mistake, the worst schism in the history of this planet. We will then see that it is our task to rectify that mistake, to throw ourselves fully into what Judaism calls *tikkun-ha'olam*, literally, "fixing up the world," repairing it. According to Jewish tradition such activity hastens the coming of the Messiah; and this corresponds to what Kefa [Peter] encourages believers in Yeshua to do, namely, to hasten the coming of the Day of God.[3] I call this approach "Olive Tree theology," after Sha'ul's [Paul's] allegory in Romans 11:16-26, addressed to Gentile Christians (my translation, from the *Jewish New Testament*):[4]

> Now if the *challah*[5] offered as firstfruits is holy, so is the whole loaf. And if the root is holy, so are the branches.

---

1   See Introduction, footnote 1.
2   For a Messianic Jewish analysis of these two theological approaches, see Dan Juster, *Jewish Roots* (2208 Rockland Ave., Rockville, Maryland 20851: Davar Publishing Co., 1986), pp. 43-45.
3   2 Kefa [2 Peter] 3:12.
4   David H. Stern, translator, *Jewish New Testament* (78 Manahat, 96901 Jerusalem, Israel and P.O. Box 1313, Clarksville, MD 21029, USA: Jewish New Testament Publications, 1989).
5   See entry on *challah* in Glossary.

But if some of the branches were broken off, and you —
a wild olive — were grafted in among them and have
become equal sharers in the rich root of the olive tree,
then don't boast as if you were better than the branches!
However, if you do boast, remember that you are not
supporting the root, the root is supporting you. So you
will say, "Branches were broken off so that I might be
grafted in." True, but so what? They were broken off
because of their lack of trust. However, you keep your
place only because of your trust. So don't be arrogant;
on the contrary, be terrified! For if God did not spare
the natural branches, he certainly won't spare you!

So take a good look at God's kindness and his severity:
on the one hand, severity toward those who fell off; but,
on the other hand, God's kindness toward you —
provided you maintain yourself in that kindness!
Otherwise, you too will be cut off! Moreover, the
others, if they do not persist in their lack of trust, will be
grafted in; because God is able to graft them back in.
For if you were cut out of what is by nature a wild olive
tree and grafted, contrary to nature, into a cultivated
olive tree, how much more will these natural branches
be grafted back into their own olive tree!

For, brothers, I want you to understand this truth
which God formerly concealed but has now revealed, so
that you won't imagine you know more than you
actually do. It is that stoniness, to a degree, has come
upon Israel, until the Gentile world enters in its fullness;
and that it is in this way that all Israel will be saved."

2. The Church And Israel In History:
Early Period.

On pages 20-21 Figure 1 depicts the "cultivated olive tree"
as it develops throughout history; while Figure 2 illustrates

cross-sections of that olive tree, showing the relationship between the Jewish people and the Church at various points in time.

The olive tree which God cultivated is Israel. Its root is the Patriarchs — Avraham, Yitzchak and Ya'akov [Abraham, Isaac and Jacob].[6] From this root grew the Jewish people. Meanwhile, the Gentiles were a wild olive tree to whom God the farmer had not devoted the same kind of special attention. Sha'ul writes that they "were at that time separated from Christ, alienated from the commonwealth of Israel, and strangers to the covenants of promise, having no hope and without God in the world."[7] Figure 2A illustrates this situation, which prevailed until the time of Yeshua's ministry (25 C.E.).

When Yeshua came, he was at the center of the tree, at the center of the Jewish people, the quintessential Jew as well as the quintessential man. He gathered Jewish disciples around him. He died, rose from the grave, and ascended to heaven. The Messianic Jewish community grew — a hundred and twenty (Acts 1:15), three thousand (Acts 2:41), five thousand (Acts 4:4), "and their numbers kept multiplying" (Acts 9:31). See Figure 2B (35 C.E.).

The non-Messianic Jews reacted against the Messianic Jews, pushing them away from the center (Acts 4-9, 12). Meanwhile, the message spread to Gentiles — Cornelius (Acts 10), Antioch (Acts 11); see Figure 2C (50 C.E.).

Although Messianic Jews in Jerusalem alone came to number "tens of thousands, ... all zealots for the Torah,"[8] Sha'ul's travels (Acts 13-28) and other missionary outreaches

---

6   "While some take $\hat{e}$ $riza$ [Greek for "the root"] to refer to Christ, and some take it to refer to the Jewish Christians, there is a very widespread agreement among commentators that it must refer to the patriarchs ..." (C. E. B. Cranfield, *Romans (International Critical Commentary)*; Edinburgh: T. & T. Clark, Ltd., 1981; volume 2, p. 565). Compare with the olive tree and its root a first-century B.C.E. Jewish source, the Book of Enoch 93:5: "And his [sc. Abraham's] posterity shall become the plant of righteousness for evermore."

7   Ephesians 2:12.

8   Acts 21:20, *Jewish New Testament*.

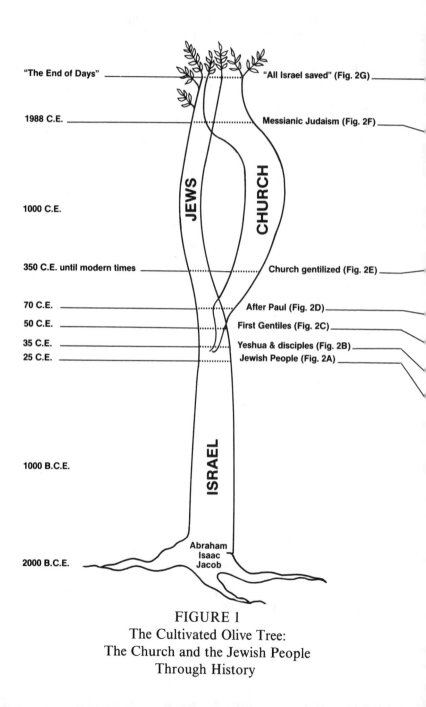

FIGURE 1
The Cultivated Olive Tree:
The Church and the Jewish People
Through History

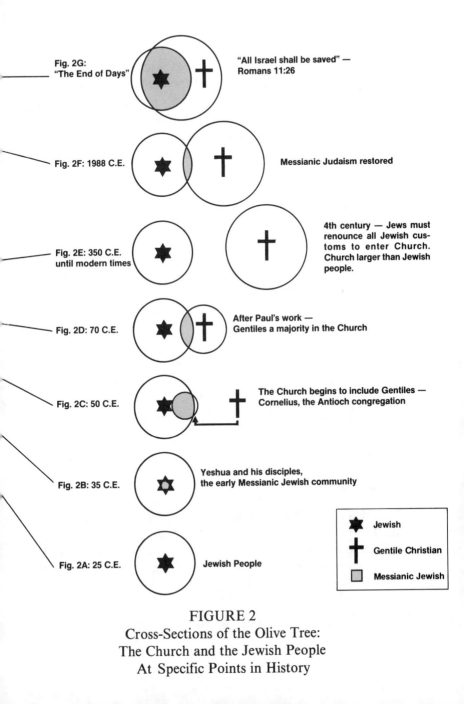

FIGURE 2
Cross-Sections of the Olive Tree:
The Church and the Jewish People
At Specific Points in History

soon made Gentiles the majority in the Church. Nevertheless, the Jewish believers were still accepted by the Jewish people as part of the Jewish community (Figure 2D, 70 C.E.).

However, by the time Sha'ul wrote the letter to the Romans (about 57 C.E.), it was clear that most Jews were rejecting Yeshua as the Messiah. Sha'ul called them branches of the cultivated olive tree which had been cut off. Yet he warned the Gentile believers that they must not take undue pride in being grafted into the olive tree or think themselves better than the cut-off branches, since they hold their position only by faith and without it will themselves be cut off. Conversely, the cut-off branches (non-Messianic Jews) can be grafted in again by faith; if anything, from an agricultural point of view, the graft is more likely to "take" with a tree's own branches than with others, and one expects the fruit from cultivated branches to be better than from wild ones (however, God is not bound by human expectations). What is important for Sha'ul is that these natural branches will in fact be grafted back in "when the Gentile world enters in its fullness."

With the passing of time, the situation for Jewish believers underwent a significant change. As the clouds gathered before the first Jewish revolt against Rome, the Messianic Jews recalled Yeshua's prophecy,

> "When you see Jerusalem surrounded by armies, then
> you are to understand that she is about to be destroyed.
> Those in Judea must escape to the hills, those inside the
> city must get out, and those in the country must not
> enter it."[9]

They fled to the city of Pella, thus escaping the destruction of the Temple (70 C.E.) and the Roman slaughter of nearly a million Jews (according to Josephus; fewer by other estimates). For this prudence the Zealots who led the rebellion regarded the Messianic Jews as traitors.

---

9   Luke 21:20-21, *Jewish New Testament.*

During the second revolt (132-135 C.E.), the Jewish
believers acquiesced initially; but when Rabbi Akiva declared
the Jewish military leader Shim'on Bar-Kochva to be the
Messiah, they could no longer cooperate, since they knew that
the Messiah is really Yeshua and could not offer allegiance to
another. This too was branded as treason, and the rest of the
Jewish community became sealed in bitterness against them.

In addition to the political tension there was also religious
tension, as witnessed by the addition to the synagogue liturgy of
the *Birkat-HaMinim* (the Benediction against the "sectarians,"
generally understood to be the Jewish believers) around 90 C.E.
In consequence of these things, the believers in Yeshua came to
be more and more excluded from the unbelieving Jewish
community.

Moreover, from the Gentile Christian side, the orthodoxy
of the Jewish believers' faith increasingly came under scrutiny if
they held to Jewish customs and loyalties. In the *Dialogue With
Trypho, A Jew*, by Justin Martyr, a Gentile Christian (about
160 C.E.), one sees a limited tolerance of Messianic Jews who
retain Jewish distinctives.[10]

---

10 Justin Martyr, "Dialogue With Trypho, A Jew" in Alexander
    Roberts and James Donaldson, editors, *The Ante-Nicene Fathers*
    (Grand Rapids, Michigan: Wm. B. Eerdmans Publishing Company,
    1975), Volume I, pp. 194-270. The following selection is from Section
    xlvii (page 218):

    If some, through weak-mindedness, wish to observe such
    institutions as were given by Moses, from which they
    expect some virtue, but which we believe were appointed
    by reason of the hardness of the people's hearts, along
    with their hope in this Christ, and [wish to perform] the
    eternal and natural acts of righteousness and piety, yet
    choose to live with the Christians and the faithful, as I said
    before, not inducing them either to be circumcised like
    themselves, or to keep the Sabbath, or to observe any
    other such ceremonies, then I hold that we ought to join
    ourselves to such, and associate with them in all things as
    kinsmen and brethren.

    He adds that he disapproves of Judaizers but believes that Judaized
    Gentile believers will be saved. However, those "who have gone back

But after Christianity became the state religion of Rome in the early fourth century, many unsaved Gentiles entered the institutional Church. It grew to be far larger than the entire Jewish population of the world, became fully Gentilized, regarded the Jews as a vanquished competitor, and had little understanding of Jewish believers who wanted to retain their Jewishness. It became impossible for a person to express publicly both Jewish and Messianic identity. A Jew who wanted to accept the Jewish Messiah had to leave his people and cross over into the Church (Figure 2E, 350 C.E.). Jews who came to faith in Yeshua were required to separate themselves utterly from Judaism, Jewish culture and the Jewish people, as we saw from the statement they had to ratify (see page 8).

That crude confession is representative — admittedly in the extreme form suited to the fanaticism of the fourth and fifth centuries — of attitudes that have persisted in the Church for hundreds of years. The Spanish Inquisition scrutinized Catholics of Jewish origin to see whether they retained Jewish customs. Out of Gentile distaste for Jewishness emerged Christian persecution of Jews — Crusades, Inquisition, pogroms, Nazi Germany (yes, there was Christian involvement, both for evil and for good) — Christian persecution of Jews, with all the pain and ugliness that Jews cannot forget, and the Church will not be permitted to forget until all Christians (not just some) learn the lesson.

So until very recently the Jewish people and the Church have remained separate, with no place for Messianic Judaism, since both the majority of Jews (unsaved people whose experience with the Church had been mostly negative) and the majority of Christians (Gentiles who misunderstood their own faith as it relates to the Jewish people) wanted it that way.

---

from some cause to the legal dispensation, and have denied that this man is Christ, and have repented not before death, shall by no means be saved."

3. Olive Tree Theology.

Leaving for a moment the historical development of this tragic division of the cultivated olive tree into two seemingly separate peoples of God, let us examine the extended metaphor of the olive tree with a view to understanding its implications for theology. There is only one cultivated tree, and that means that there is only one Israel, not two. The wild branches (Gentiles) have been grafted in through faith in the Messiah, "brought near in the blood of Christ,"[11] so that they are now included in the commonwealth of Israel. But they are not, as Replacement theology would have it, a New Israel. Nor do Jewish and Gentile believers together constitute a New Israel, since the cut-off branches too are still identifiable as Israel even though they do not have the living sap of the tree flowing through them. For God is miraculously preserving them, so that instead of drying out, as detached branches normally do, they are able to be grafted back in by faith. Thus unsaved Jews (cut-off natural branches), saved Jews (natural branches attached to the tree), and Gentile believers (grafted-in wild branches) each have their own kind of ongoing participation in the one Israel; and this fact needs to be taken into account in any correct theology of Israel and the Church.

Not a word is said in the "olive tree" passage or anywhere else in Scripture about splitting the promises into earthly ones for the Jews and heavenly ones for the Church. However, God has made two kinds of promises. In regard to the promises which relate to individual salvation, there is neither Jew nor Gentile (Galatians 3:28), no distinction between them (Romans 10:12), no dividing wall of hostility (Ephesians 2:14-19). On the other hand, there remain promises to national Israel, the Jewish people, in which Gentile nations corporately and Gentile believers individually have no direct share — although it is worth noting that there are also promises to certain Gentile nations (as an example, Isaiah 19:24-25 gives assurance that

---

11 Ephesians 2:13.

God will bless Egypt and Assyria along with Israel; so that Gentile believers who are part of those nations will experience those blessings).

The present situation with commonwealth Israel is that Gentiles from many nations recognize the Jewish Messiah, yet the majority of national Israel do not. Suppose citizens of Canada, India, Nigeria, Australia, and other members of the British Commonwealth of Nations recognized Elizabeth II as their Queen, but most individual Englishmen, as well as the British government, did not. In this circumstance it would be wrong to say that Great Britain was no longer a member of the Commonwealth — when in fact it would still be the central member among equals. It would also be incorrect to agree with the English that Elizabeth is not the Queen. Rather, one could only try to convince them — both individual Englishmen and their governmental establishment — to honor Elizabeth II, who is in fact the Queen.[12]

4. The Church And Israel In History: Modern Period.

In the future, "all Israel will be saved." In the *Tanakh*, that is to say, in Hebrew thinking, the word *kol* ("all") in reference to a collective does not mean every single individual of which it is composed, but rather the main part, the essential part, the considerable majority. Therefore I believe that when "all Israel" is saved, it will not be that every Jew believes in Yeshua, but that the Jewish nation will have a believing majority and/or a believing establishment. To use Moses' metaphor, the Messianic Jews will be "the head and not the tail."[13] (See Figure 2G.)

I believe that the reappearance of a Messianic Jewish community in our day is a significant phase in God's process of

---

12   I am indebted to Daniel Juster, *Growing To Maturity*, ([Gaithersburg, Maryland: Union of Messianic Jewish Congregations], 1982), pp. 253-254, for this analogy.
13   Deuteronomy 28:13.

saving all Israel. If Figure 2G is the ultimate goal, and Figure 2E shows the situation as it actually existed until recently, then Figure 2D not only depicts an ancient historical stage, but also resembles the present and the immediate future, represented by Figure 2F, showing that we are beginning to recover our past. It has once again become possible for a Jewish believer in Yeshua to identify himself as both Jewish and Messianic, and to express this identification in a socially recognizable way. This has come about historically because of the great growth of freedom in Western political, economic and social life during the last three hundred years, a phenomenon which surely demonstrates God's love for humanity. Previously a tiny minority could not have hoped to effect fundamental change in two much larger opposed social entities by claiming to be part of both. Today our freedom to attempt this outrageously improbable task (improbable by the world's standards but not by God's) is protected in pluralistic democratic countries. As political freedom grew, already by 1718 John Toland in his book *Nazarenus*[14] could suggest that "Christians . . . from among the Jews" should observe the Torah. As economic freedom grew, the Hebrew Christian movement could advance with few impediments in nineteenth-century England. And as social freedom has grown, along with the advance in communications, it is possible for us, today, to dare expect that Messianic Judaism will succeed in reaching its goal of healing the split between the Church and the Jewish people.

It is the task of Messianic Jews and of sympathetic Gentile Christians to undertake the *tikkun-ha'olam* of which we spoke earlier. These are the ones who, because of their common trust in the Jewish Messiah Yeshua, can work together to undo the damage caused by the division of the Jewish people and the

---

14 John Toland, *Nazarenus*, 1718; quoted in both David Rausch, *Messianic Judaism: Its History, Theology and Polity* (New York and Toronto: The Edwin Mellen Press, 1982), pp. 51-54 and Hugh Schonfield, *The History of Jewish Christianity* (London: Duckworth, 1936), pp. 205-208.

Church into two apparently separate peoples of God. The Jewish people must be brought to understand — freely, willingly, not by coercion or deception — that the age-old goals of Jewish endeavor will be achieved only when the Jewish people come to understand and trust in Yeshua, the Jewish Messiah. The Church must be brought to understand — freely, willingly, not by coercion or deception — that its goals will be achieved only when any form of overt or covert antisemitism or stand-offishness has disappeared, and intimate unity with the Jewish people has been acknowledged.

Can there be a grander goal? We live in an exciting age, as we see the momentum of history sweeping toward the fulfillment of Sha'ul's prophecy that all Israel will be saved. And as we work toward accomplishing that end, it is essential that we be armed with a right understanding of the relationship between Israel and the Church.

C. The Gospel Is Corporate As Well As Individual.

There are aspects of the Gospel which are corporate, not just related to individuals. Christians who understand that it is right to preach the Gospel to Jews often offer a Gospel which is inadequate because it is oriented only toward the individual and does not deal with the Jewish people as a corporate entity. In my view a gospel only for individuals is inadequate not only for Jews, but for Gentiles as well.

What is the Gospel for the individual? The New Testament's most complete statement of it, as we suggested in the Introduction, is in Sha'ul's letter to the Romans, Chapters 1-8 — although every essential part can be found in the *Tanakh*. Chapters 1-3 tell us that everyone has sinned and falls short of obeying God adequately (1 Kings 8:46, Ecclesiastes 7:20), that this sin builds a wall between him and God (Isaiah 59:1-2), that the penalty for sin is death (Genesis 2:17), and that no one can restore the relationship with God by his own efforts (Psalm 143:2, Isaiah 64:5-6), but that God, from his side, by his own sovereign act of offering Yeshua the Messiah as an atonement for sin, has bridged the gap and restored fellowship between the individual and his God (Isaiah 52:13-53:12). Chapters 4-6 explain that what a person must do to have his own individual relationship with God restored is to put his trust in God, accepting personally what God has already done for him through Yeshua (Genesis 15:6). Chapters 7-8 add that such trust from the heart, which the New Testament makes clear is not merely intellectual affirmation of certain facts (Ya'akov [James] 2:14-26), will lead to his both wanting and being able — by the power of the Holy Spirit in him — to do those deeds which are pleasing to God.

In America, where the individual's right to pursue his own happiness has for more than two centuries been regarded as virtually a law of nature (what the Declaration of Independence called an "inalienable right"), the Gospel for the individual is conveniently presented in little booklets containing four or five "spiritual laws;" and it is possible to suppose that that's all there is to the Gospel. But salvation is corporate, for the community as well as for the individual. Any study of the word *yeshu'ah* ("salvation, deliverance") in the Hebrew Bible will show that deliverance is never thought of as being for the individual alone, although individual salvation definitely is part of the Old Testament message.[15] Nevertheless salvation for the individual Jew apart from concern for the deliverance of the Jewish people as a whole is simply not found in the *Tanakh*. On the contrary, much of its discussion of salvation is focussed on the integrity and holiness of the Jewish people as a whole, witness, for example, the frequent explanation in Deuteronomy for capital punishment or excommunication, "so that the evil may be purged from among you."[16]

Since most Jewish people, after 4,000 years of communal

15   See Psalm 51:12 (51:14 in some versions).
16   In this context note also the story of Achan in Joshua 7.

history, have a strong sense of peoplehood,[17] an individual Gospel seems to them both selfish and inadequate, since it does not touch directly on national and universal aspirations. On average, Jews live more corporately than most individualistic Westerners — and I say this to the shame of the Church, which the New Testament proclaims to be "one body." Indeed, the Church can and should learn from the Jewish people what it means to care for one another.

To put this idea another way, my individual tie to God is direct, yet it is not alone — it is intertwined with yours. A Gospel which ignores the intertwining of lives together in "nations and kindreds and people and tongues"[18] is overly simple, escapist. "No man is an island, entire of itself." Scriptural religion is not practiced in the lotus position. Not only will an overly inward-directed Gospel fail to attract people more attuned to the good of society, which many Jewish people are, but it fails to represent fully the concerns of God.

For Gentiles, who must be saved in spite of their culture and religious background, one could argue that the individual aspect is the key. This is why Sha'ul, the Emissary to the Gentiles[19] emphasized it so much. Likewise, the individual

---

17   See, for example, Mordechai M. Kaplan, *The Greater Judaism In The Making* (New York: The Reconstructionist Press, 1960), especially the page references under "Jewish peoplehood" in the index. A sample, from pp. 30-31:

> The Jewish people seem to have achieved a more intense and permanent ethnic consciousness than any other ancient people. ... The entire education of the Jewish child was confined to writings which dealt with the Jewish people. The main purpose of that education was to cultivate in him a loyalty and devotion to Israel and Israel's God, and to teach him the facts he had to know and the duties he had to perform as a member of the Jewish people. ... [Communion with God in worship] was not in terms of an I-Thou but of a We-Thou relationship, the 'We' being the Jewish people which God had chosen to make Him known to all the world."

18   Revelation 7:9.
19   Romans 11:14.

aspects of the Gospel may speak adequately to the hearts of assimilated or troubled Jews whose involvement with the Jewish community is weak. But Jews who feel part and parcel of their people — and not a few socially oriented Gentiles as well — need to hear the corporate aspects of the Gospel too, or they may dismiss it as shallow and not get saved.

Moreover, even people whose interest is their own personal well-being need to hear the corporate aspects of the Gospel. In fact, they need it even more, since a major aspect of salvation for them may involve turning from a selfish, egocentric approach to life and adopting God's approach to life, which is oriented toward others.[20] Thus a Gospel lacking a focus on corporate and societal elements fails to be "the whole counsel of God"[21] for anyone.

D. Yeshua Is Identified With The People Of Israel.

An interesting way to think about the Gospel as simultaneously individual and corporate is to consider the ways in which the Messiah Yeshua stands for and is intimately identified with his people Israel. Just as the individual who trusts Yeshua becomes united with him and is "immersed" (baptized) into all that Yeshua is, including his death and resurrection — so that his sin nature is regarded as dead, and his new nature, empowered by the Holy Spirit, is regarded as alive — just as this intimate identification with the Messiah holds for the individual, so the Messiah similarly identifies with and embodies national Israel.

In the New Testament one encounters this notion first at Mattityahu [Matthew] 2:15, where it is said of Yeshua's being taken to Egypt, "This happened in order to fulfill what *Adonai* had said through the prophet, 'Out of Egypt I called my son.'" The verse quoted is Hosea 11:1. However, in context the

---

20 Leviticus 19:18, Philippians 2:1-11.
21 Acts 20:27.

prophet Hosea was clearly speaking not about a future Messiah but about the nation of Israel and the Exodus.

Some accuse Mattityahu of misusing Scripture here, recklessly taking a verse out of context and applying it to Yeshua. Is he guilty? To answer, we should take note of the four kinds of Scripture interpretation which the rabbis used:

* *P'shat* ("simple") — The plain, simple sense of the text, what modern interpreters call grammatical-historical exegesis.

* *Remez* ("hint") — Peculiar features of the text are regarded as hinting at a deeper truth than that conveyed by its plain sense.

* *Drash* or *midrash* ("search") — Creativity is used to search the text in relation to the rest of the Bible, other literature or life in order to develop an allegorical or homiletical application of the text. This involves eisegesis — reading one's own thoughts into a text — as well as exegesis, which is extracting from a text its actual meaning.

* *Sod* ("secret") — One operates on the numerical values of the Hebrew letters; for example, two words whose letters add up to the same amount would be good candidates for revealing a secret through "bisociation of ideas."[22]

The accusation that Mattityahu is misappropriating Scripture stands only if he is dealing with the *p'shat*. For as we have said, the *p'shat* of Hosea 11:1 applies to the nation of Israel and not to Yeshua.

But perhaps Mattityahu is making a *midrash*, reading the Messiah into a verse dealing with Israel? Many rabbis used the same approach; his readers would not have found it objectionable.

---

22 The term was coined by Arthur Koestler, the assimilated Jewish cosmopolitan political philosopher and novelist, in his book, *The Act Of Creation* (1964).

Nevertheless, I believe Mattityahu is doing neither but giving us a *remez*, a hint of a very deep truth. Israel is called God's son as far back as Exodus 4:22. The Messiah is presented as God's son a few verses earlier in Mattityahu 1:18-25, reflecting *Tanakh* passages such as Isaiah 9:6-7, Psalm 2:7 and Proverbs 30:4. Thus the Son equals the son; the Messiah is equated with the nation of Israel. This is what Mattityahu is hinting at by calling Yeshua's flight to Egypt a "fulfillment" of Hosea 11:1.

The idea that one stands for all can be found throughout the Bible, sometimes for weal and sometimes for woe — in the story of Achan's sin (Joshua 7), in the relationship between Israel and her king (many places in the *Tanakh*, for example, 1 Kings 9:3-9), in Romans 5:12-21, in 1 Corinthians 15:45-49, and in the debate over the "servant passages" of Isaiah (42:1-9, 49:1-13, 50:4-11, and 52:11-53:12). In fact, the controversy over whether Isaiah 53 refers to Israel or to a then unborn Messiah dissolves when it is remembered that Israel's Messiah embodies his people. Likewise, consider these phrases from Isaiah 49:1-6:

> "Adonai ... said to me, 'You are my servant, Israel, in whom I will be glorified.' ... And now Adonai says, ... 'It is too light a thing that you should be my servant, to raise up the tribes of Jacob and to restore the preserved of Israel; I will give you as a light to the nations, that my salvation may reach to the end of the earth.'"

Does Israel restore the preserved of Israel? Who is the "light to the nations"? Judaism understands this as a goal to be fulfilled by the Jewish people. Christians think at once of Yochanan [John] 8:12, where Yeshua said of himself, "I am the light of the world." I suggest that the Jewish people will be the light to the nations that we ought to be when we have in us him who is the light of the world.

This concept, that the Messiah embodies the Jewish people, should not seem strange to believers, who learn precisely that about Yeshua and the Church. What else does it mean to talk of the Church as a body of which the Messiah is the head? Or a temple of which he is the chief cornerstone? The concept of one standing for all is familiar. But the Church has not clearly grasped that the Holy One of Israel, Yeshua, is in union not only with the Church, but also with the Jewish people. When Christians have fully digested this and can communicate to Jews that through Yeshua the Messiah, by virtue of his identification with Israel, the Jewish people will achieve their destiny, then the Jewish people will have been presented a less alien and more attractive Gospel. And the Church will have become more faithful to it.

"The truth, the whole truth, and nothing but the truth"? Yeshua said, "I am ... the truth." But he identifies with Israel. A believer in the Gospel acquires truth by identifying with Yeshua. But if so, he too, whether Jewish or Gentile, must identify with the Jewish people, with whom Yeshua identifies. Otherwise he has not identified with Yeshua. That's the truth! "Ye shall know the truth" — Yeshua, who identifies with the Jewish people — "and the truth shall make you free."[23]

E. God Will Fulfill His Promises To The Jewish People.

A major corporate element in the Good News is the guarantee that God will fulfill his promises to the Jewish people as a people. These promises appear in the *Tanakh* over and over; two of the most important of them are that the Jewish people will return from Exile to possess and inhabit *Eretz-Yisrael* [the Land of Israel], and that the Kingdom will be re-established with the Son of David on the throne.

1. The New Testament Proves It.

Many Christians are unaware that the New Testament affirms

---

23   Yochanan [John] 8:32.

the future fulfillment of God's promises to national Israel. We shall examine two texts by way of demonstration.

The first is Mattityahu [Matthew] 23:37-39. After excoriating a particular group of *Torah*-teachers ["scribes"] and *P'rushim* ["Pharisees"] whose hardened hearts had turned against spiritual truth, Yeshua exclaimed,

> "Jerusalem! Jerusalem! You kill the prophets! You stone those who are sent to you! How often I wanted to gather your children, just as a hen gathers her chickens under her wings, but you refused! Look! 'God is abandoning your house to you, leaving it desolate.' [Jeremiah 22:5] For I tell you, from now on, you will not see me again until you say, 'Blessed is he who comes in the name of *Adonai.*'" [Psalm 118:26]

Regardless of whether the Messiah calling "Jerusalem! Jerusalem!" is addressing all Jewish people or only the Jewish establishment centered in the Holy City, it is obvious that he is speaking not just to individuals but to the nation as a whole, promising that national salvation will come to Israel when she says, as a nation, "Blessed is he who comes in the name of the Lord."

Another key passage affirming that God will fulfill his promises to national Israel is Romans 9-11. This section of the Book of Romans is not, as some extreme Dispensationalists claim, a "parenthesis" unrelated to what Sha'ul writes before and after. Rather, it answers a key question raised by the last verses of Chapter 8, where Sha'ul promises that believers in Yeshua, having been chosen, will be glorified (v. 30), and that nothing can prevent it (vv. 31-39). The natural response of the first-century reader to this assurance that God will keep his promises to anyone who has faith must have been, "What about Israel? I don't see God keeping his promises to them. The Messiah came and went, and the Jewish people are not following him. What about Israel?" The answer of Romans 9-11 is that God will indeed keep his promises to Israel — in his own way and in his own time — so that in the end, "all Israel," that is, Israel as a national entity, "will be saved."

Thus we see that the future of national Israel is indeed mentioned in the New Testament; moreover, these two passages are by no means the only places.

2. The Tanakh Proves It

Even if the New Testament had made no mention of promises to the Jewish nation, we would still have them as stated in the *Tanakh*, which is, after all, still the Word of God. What Christians call the Old Testament was Yeshua's only Bible, and he believed it with all his heart. In fact, referring to the *Tanakh* and its promises, he said, "Scripture cannot be broken." Likewise Sha'ul wrote that "All Scripture," *i.e.*, the entire *Tanakh*, "is inspired by God and is profitable for doctrine. . . ."[24] The New Testament does not cancel or replace the *Tanakh*; rather, it is built upon it — or, more accurately, assumes it. That is, everything written in the *Tanakh* is assumed by the New Testament to be faithful and true, including all the promises to national Israel.

Moreover, the *Tanakh*'s promises of a New Covenant and a new heart and spirit for the Jewish people are coupled with the promise that they will remain a nation and will live safely in the Land of Israel (Jeremiah 31:30-37 and Ezekiel 36:22-36). If we believe that the prophecies of a New Covenant found in these passages are fulfilled by Yeshua, we should also believe that the associated prophecies of Israel's return from Exile to the Land will also be fulfilled. The Bible does not allow itself to be cut in pieces according to the reader's preconceived notions.

3. Refutation Of Arguments That God Is Finished With The Jews.

Yet there are those whose theology does not admit that there remain promises to the Jewish nation as such. In fact, most

---

24   Yochanan [John] 10:35, 2 Timothy 3:16.

forms of Replacement theology say that when the Jewish people failed to accept Yeshua as the Messiah, they forfeited all the blessings of the Old Covenant, and what remains to them as a people is only the curses. We have already indicated that Replacement theology is based on a wrong understanding of the relationship between Israel and the Church;[25] but because its influence is great, we will analyze two New Testament verses which it uses to deny God's promises to the Jewish people, demonstrating instead that these verses actually confirm them.

a. 2 Corinthians 1:20

"For all the promises of God find their Yes in him," that is, in Yeshua.

Replacement theology understands this to mean that all the Old Testament promises have in some mystical sense been fulfilled in the Messiah already, so that none remain for the Jews. But the verse does not say or mean that all the promises have been fulfilled already, but that whenever God's promises are fulfilled, they are fulfilled in, through or by Yeshua. He is the instrument through whom God the Father has fulfilled, is fulfilling and will fulfill every promise he has ever made to the Jewish people — including the promise that they will return from Exile to possess and live in the Land of Israel and the promise that the Kingdom will be restored, with the Son of David on the throne. A text which assures that God will fulfill every one of his promises to the Jews must not be turned into a pretext for cancelling them!

b. Mattityahu [Matthew] 5:17

"Do not think that I came to abolish the Law or the Prophets; I did not come to abolish, but to fulfill."

Replacement theology likewise understands that Yeshua at his first coming fulfilled the *Torah*, so that we don't have to do so (the logic leading to this conclusion is unclear); and that he

---

25 On Replacement theology, see Section B-1 above and footnote 1.

fulfilled all the Old Testament prophecies, so that, once again, none remain for the Jews.

But the word usually translated "fulfill", Greek *pleroô*, does not necessarily convey this specific sense. Rather, it is a very common word which simply means "fill", "fill up", "make full", as in filling a cup or a hole. It should be evident that the actual meaning is as rendered in the *Jewish New Testament*: "Don't think that I have come to abolish the *Torah* or the Prophets. I have come not to abolish but to complete" — that is, to "make full" the meaning of what the *Torah* and the ethical demands of the Prophets require. In fact, this verse, so understood, states the theme of the entire Sermon on the Mount — in which six times the Messiah says, "You have heard of old time" the incomplete meaning or a distortion, "but I say to you" the complete, full spiritual sense to be understood and obeyed.

As with 2 Corinthians 1:20, Yeshua does fulfill the predictions of the Prophets; likewise, he kept the *Torah* perfectly. But that is not what Yeshua is talking about here in the Sermon on the Mount. He will indeed fulfill every unfulfilled prophecy concerning himself, and he will also be the means by which God the Father will cause to be fulfilled every as yet unfulfilled prophecy concerning the Jews.

To sum up, the Hebrew Bible's promises to the Jews are not cancelled in the name of being "fulfilled in Yeshua." Rather, fulfillment in Yeshua is an added assurance that what God has promised the Jews will yet come to pass. "For the gifts and the call of God are irrevocable."[26]

4. The Promise Of The Land.

Certainly one of the most important aspects of the Jewish Gospel is the promise that Israel will return from the Exile to

---

26   Romans 11:29. Sha'ul writes this strong word of assurance when discussing the promise that "all Israel shall be saved" (Romans 11:26). But this great overarching promise to the Jewish people subsumes the entire panoply of promises God made to them in the Hebrew Bible.

Eretz-Yisrael. True, not every Jew thinks of his Diaspora existence as Exile. Many Jews regard America (or whatever country they happen to live in) as flowing with more milk and honey than the Promised Land. But God presents in his Word a contrary opinion, and it is his opinion which will in the end prevail. In the manner and time of his choosing, God will gather Jewish people from the nations of the earth back to the Land which he gave them "as an inheritance forever."[27]

Of course, this promise is rooted in the *Tanakh*; but an interesting New Testament reference to the Land is in the Olivet Discourse, where most translations distort the meaning. According to Mattityahu [Matthew] 24:30, when the sign of the Son of Man appears in the sky, "all the tribes of the Land will mourn" — *not* "all the tribes of the earth," as in most versions, because Yeshua is alluding to Zechariah 12:10, 14. Mattityahu comes to tell us that when the Messiah returns "on the clouds of heaven, with tremendous power and glory," the twelve tribes of Israel will be living in the Land of Israel, and they will see him.

Replacement theology sometimes bases its view that there is no longer any valid Jewish claim to the Land of Israel on the notion that with the coming of Yeshua the Mosaic Covenant, with its promise of the Land, was abolished. Although I do not agree that this covenant has been abolished any more than the Abrahamic one has, it is useful to point out that the promise of the Land predates Moses. This promise was made to Abraham (Genesis 12:7, 13:14-17, 15:7-21, 17:7-8, 24:7), Isaac (Genesis 26:2-4; 28:3-4, 13-15) and Jacob (Genesis 35:11-12), long before Moses came on the scene, although the promise was repeated to him as well (Exodus 32:13). By the logic of Galatians 3:15-17, which says that a later covenant does not alter an earlier one, the promise of the Land made to the Patriarchs is altered neither by the coming of the New Covenant nor by the supposed abrogation of the Mosaic one.[28]

---

27   See references to Genesis and Exodus in text, two paragraphs below.
28   This seems an appropriate place for a word about how the Letter To

Today, when the issue of who has which rights to the Land of Israel is constantly in the newspapers, Christians need to know what the Bible says. Let them not be taken in by Colin Chapman's book, *Whose Promised Land?*,[29] which uses Replacement theology as its basis for denying that the Land of Israel is any longer promised by God to the Jews.

On the contrary, I like a formula suggested to me by Joseph Shulam, leader of the "Netivyah" Congregation in Jerusalem:

A Group Of Messianic Jews ["To The Hebrews"] deals with the "old" and "new" covenants.

> For if the system of *cohanim* is transformed, there must of necessity occur a transformation of *Torah*. ... Thus, on the one hand, the earlier rule is set aside because of its weakness and inefficacy (for the *Torah* did not bring anything to the goal); and, on the other hand, a hope of something better is introduced, through which we are drawing near to God. (Messianic Jews 7:12, 18-19, *Jewish New Testament*)

The transformation of *Torah* does not imply its abolition. Specific rules are set aside — for example, the *Torah* has to be adjusted to take account of Yeshua's role as *cohen gadol* (high priest). But the *Torah* itself continues and is to be observed. (For more on this, see below, Section F.)

> "See! The days are coming," says *Adonai*, "when I will establish ... a new covenant. ..." [Jeremiah 31:30-34] By using the term, "new," he has made the first covenant "old"; and something being made old, something in the process of aging, is close to vanishing altogether. (Messianic Jews 8:9, 13, *JNT*)

Yeshua's second coming is close (I Corinthians 7:29-31), but it has not happened yet (2 Thessalonians 2:1-2). Likewise, although the old covenant is "close to vanishing," it has not yet vanished. We do not know when it will vanish; perhaps it will be after Yeshua returns. In the meantime, the Mosaic Covenant is here to be observed and not broken from our side (even though our fathers did break it — Jeremiah 31:31-32, Messianic Jews 8:10), since it has never been broken from God's side. (For more on this see my *Messianic Jewish Manifesto* (*op. cit.* in Chapter I, footnote 3), Chapter IV, Section E-1; also see below, Section F-2-d.)

29 Colin Chapman, *Whose Promised Land?* (Tring, Herts, England: Lion Publishing, 1983).

"Although the Arabs do not have the right *to* the Land, they do have rights *in* the Land." God has promised governance over *Eretz-Yisrael* to the Jewish people, but the "dwellers in the Land" have the right to peaceful and undisturbed use of property to which they have title, the right to be paid a fair price for land purchased from them, the right not to be exploited or shamed or mistreated. We Israeli Jews who are currently ruling the Arabs in the Territories by a military administration have no better guide to behavior than the *Torah* and the Prophets:

> For *Adonai* your God is God of gods and Lord of lords, the great, the mighty, the awesome God. He is not partial and he takes no bribe; he executes justice for the fatherless and the widow; he loves the sojourner, giving him food and clothing. Therefore, you are to love the sojourner, for you were sojourners in the land of Egypt.[30]

> He has shown you, O man, what is good — and what does the Lord require of you except to do justice, love kindness, and walk humbly with your God?[31]

While on the subject, let me say a few words about peace between Jews and Arabs. There are Jews who despair of achieving any sort of peaceful coexistence with Arabs, and there are others who make efforts at contact and understanding. It seems to me that the one great hope for genuine peace with justice lies in loving fellowship between Arab Christians and Messianic Jews based on our common faith in Yeshua (in Arabic, *Yesua*). Only the Messiah in the hearts of Arabs and Jews can make peace between us. There are efforts being made in this direction right now. The path is long, the dangers and opportunities for mistakes are many; yet I can see no other hope. The enmity between Jews and Arabs has theological overtones which only our common trust in the

---

30   Deuteronomy 10:17-19.
31   Micah 6:8.

Messiah has any possibility of bridging. For the Jews are God's measuring stick — "I will bless those who bless you and curse him who curses you," said God to Abraham,[32] and this applies to Arabs too. On the other hand, God reserved blessings for Ishmael: he would make him a "great nation."[33]

The efforts at fellowship between Arabs and Jews to date are promising, hopeful, moving. Still, we have far to go. We sing each other's songs, and we rejoice in each other's testimonies of coming to faith. But we have yet to pour out our hurts to each other, to acknowledge and repent of our sins, to forgive and to seek forgiveness, to reveal our inmost desires. We also have yet to submit our own ideas on the Land to each other and to the discipline of Scripture, with the object of reaching theological agreement. Pray for us in these areas.

And as for politics? Hawks? Doves? War? Peace? I believe with perfect faith that if enough Jews and enough Arabs are won to putting their trust in Yeshua, the King of Israel, and submitting to him, there will be peace.

The present State of Israel is obviously not the Messianic state, but it appears to be a phase of *tikkun-ha'olam*. Joseph Shulam, using the *Tanakh*'s principle of the "faithful remnant," has taught that God protects the State of Israel for the sake of its Messianic Jews, who constitute the present-day remnant of Israel. Yeshua called believers "the salt of the Land,"[34] salt being a preservative, so that one might say the Messianic Jews preserve the State of Israel in the Land of Israel.

5. *The Promise Of The Kingdom.*

God promised that there would always be a descendant of David to rule the Jewish people.[35] As is well known, the popular expectation at the time of Yeshua was that the Messiah would

---

32   Genesis 12:3.
33   Genesis 21:13.
34   Mattityahu [Matthew] 5:13; in most translations, "the salt of the earth."
35   2 Samuel 7:14.

restore the national fortunes of Israel, freeing her from the Roman yoke and re-establishing the kingship. So anxious were some of Yeshua's hearers to have this dream fulfilled that they tried to achieve it by force.[36]

During his three-year ministry Yeshua kept his disciples from pestering him about it by teaching them that he had to die for the sins of mankind and rise from the dead. But when he had accomplished these things it was not unreasonable for them to ask him,

> "Lord, are you at this time going to restore self-rule to Israel?" He answered, "You don't need to know the dates or the times; the Father has kept these under his own authority."[37]

His answer may not have been what they wanted to hear, but we do learn from this New Testament text that *whether* God will "restore self-rule to Israel" is not in question. The only uncertainty is *when*.

6. Conclusion.

In conclusion, the promises of God to the Jewish nation are a key element in biblical religion. Who knows whether without them the Jewish people would have survived? They remain central to Jewish community life. A Gospel which has nothing to say about them is a Gospel few committed Jews can consider. Fortunately, as we have seen, the real Gospel, the Jewish Gospel of Yeshua the Messiah, confirms those promises; indeed, it is through him that they are all Yes.

F. The Role Of *Torah* In The Gospel.

1. Torah Incognita.

I am certain that the lack of a correct, clear and relatively complete Messianic Jewish or Gentile Christian theology of the

---

36 Yochanan [John] 6:15.
37 Acts 1:6-7, *Jewish New Testament.*

Law is not only a major impediment to Christians' understanding their own faith, but also the greatest barrier to Jewish
people's receiving the Gospel. Even though many Jews do not
observe *Torah*, often neither knowing nor caring about it, I
stand by this statement; because Jewish attachment to the
Torah lies buried deep in the racial memory, often affecting
attitudes unconsciously.

While ultimately the issue becomes who Yeshua is —
Messiah, Son of the Living God, final Atonement, Lord of our
lives — the Church's problem here is mainly one of communication, of expressing the truth in ways that relate to Jewish
world-views. But the Church hardly knows what to make of the
Torah, or how to fit it together with the New Testament. And if
the Church doesn't know, don't expect the Jews to figure it out
for them! I believe that Christianity has gone far astray in its
dealings with the subject and that the most urgent task of
theology today is get right its view of the Law.

Christianity organizes systematic theology by subjects it
considers important. Thus topics like the Holy Spirit and the
person and work of the Messiah take a healthy amount of space
in any Christian systematic theology. Judaism too organizes its
theological thinking into categories reflecting its concerns, and
perusal of treatises on Judaism reveals that its three main
themes are God, Israel (that is, the Jewish people) and *Torah*.

Comparing Jewish and Christian theology, one finds that
both devote much attention to God and to the people of God (in
the one case the Jews, in the other the Church). It is all the more
striking, therefore, to notice how much Jewish thought and
how little Christian theology addresses the topic of *Torah* —
generally rendered in English as "Law," although the meaning
of the Hebrew word is "teaching." As a rough measure, I
checked the subject index of Augustus Strong's *Systematic
Theology* and found under "Law" 28 pages out of a total of
1,056 (less than 3%). In L. Berkhof's *Systematic Theology* there
are 3 pages out of 745 (less than 1/2 %). And in Lewis Sperry
Chafer's 7-volume work with the same title, there are only 7 out

of 2,607 (about 1/4%). On the other hand, Isidor Epstein's *The Faith of Judaism* has 57 pages on *Torah* out of 386 (15%), Solomon Schechter's *Aspects of Rabbinic Theology* has 69 out of 343 (20%), and Louis Jacobs' *A Jewish Theology* 73 out of 331 (22%) (these three authors are Orthodox, Conservative and Liberal (Reform), respectively). One is forced to the conclusion that the topic interests Jews and not Christians.

And that is unfortunate for the Christians. It means, first, that most Christians have an overly simplistic understanding of what the Law is all about; and, second, that Christianity has almost nothing relevant to say to Jews about one of the three most important issues of their faith. In short, *Torah* is the great unexplored territory, the *terra incognita* of Christian theology.

The main reason for this is that Christian theology, with the anti-Jewish bias it incorporated in its early centuries, misunderstood Sha'ul and concluded that the *Torah* is no longer in force. This is not the Jewish Gospel, nor is it the true Gospel. It is time for Christians to understand the truth about the Law. Christian theologians in the last thirty years have made a beginning.[38] Messianic Jews should now move to the front lines and spearhead this process.

2. Nomos.

A good starting place would be a thorough study of the Greek word *nomos* ("law," *"Torah"*) and its derivatives as used in the New Testament. Unfortunately there is not space in this book

---

38 See W. D. Davies, *Paul And Rabbinic Judaism*, 4th ed. (Philadelphia: Fortress Press, 1980); Daniel P. Fuller, *Gospel And Law: Contrast Or Continuum?* (Grand Rapids, Michigan: Eerdmans, 1980); Hans Huebner, *Law In Paul's Thought* (Edinburgh: T. & T. Clark, 1984); Jacob Jervell, *The Unknown Paul* (Minneapolis: Augsburg Press, 1984); E. P. Sanders, *Paul, The Law, And The Jewish People* (Philadelphia: Fortress Press, 1983); E. P. Sanders, *Paul And Palestinian Judaism* (London: SCM Press, Ltd., 1977); Gerard S. Sloyan, *Is Christ The End Of The Law?* (Philadelphia: Westminster Press, 1978); Clark M. Williamson, *Has God Rejected His People?* (Nashville, Tennessee: Abingdon, 1982).

to undertake it, since the word and its cognates appear some 200 times. The sampling which follows is intended to whet the appetite and encourage further investigation.

a. Romans 10:4 — Did The Messiah End The Law?

Consider Romans 10:4, which states — in a typical but wrong translation — "For Christ ends the law and brings righteousness for everyone who has faith." Like this translator, most theologians understand the verse to say that Yeshua terminated the *Torah*. But the Greek word translated "ends" is *telos*, from which English gets the word "teleology," defined in Webster's Third International Dictionary as "the philosophical study of the evidences of design in nature; . . . the fact or the character of being directed toward an end or shaped by a purpose — used of . . . nature . . . conceived as determined . . . by the design of a divine Providence. . . ." The normal meaning of *telos* in Greek — which is also its meaning here — is "goal, purpose, consummation," not "termination." The Messiah did not and does not bring the *Torah* to an end. Rather, attention to and faith in the Messiah is the goal and purpose toward which the *Torah* aims, the logical consequence, result and consummation of observing the *Torah* out of genuine faith (as opposed to trying to observe it out of legalism). This, not the termination of *Torah* is Sha'ul's point, as can be seen from the context, Romans 9:30-10:11.

b. "Under The Law" and "Works Of The Law".

Much of Christian theology about the *Torah* is based on a misunderstanding of two Greek expressions which Sha'ul invented. The first is *upo nomon*; it appears 10 times in Romans, 1 Corinthians and Galatians, and it is usually rendered "under the law." The other is *erga nomou*, found with minor variations 10 times in Romans and Galatians, translated "works of the law."

Whatever Sha'ul is trying to communicate by these expressions, one thing is clear: Sha'ul regards them negatively:

being "under the law" is bad, and "works of the law" are bad. Christian theology usually takes the first to mean "within the framework of observing the *Torah*" and the second, "acts of obedience to the *Torah*." This understanding is wrong. Sha'ul does not consider it bad to live within the framework of *Torah*, nor is it bad to obey it; on the contrary, he writes that the *Torah* is "holy, just and good" (Romans 7:12).

C. E. B. Cranfield has shed light on these two phrases; his first essay on the subject appeared in 1964,[39] and he summarized it in his masterly commentary on Romans.[40] There he writes,

> . . .the Greek language of Paul's day possessed no word-group corresponding to our "legalism", "legalist" and "legalistic". This means that he lacked a convenient terminology for expressing a vital distinction, and so was surely seriously hampered in the work of clarifying the Christian position with regard to the law. In view of this, we should always, we think, be ready to reckon with the possibility that Pauline statements, which at first sight seem to disparage the law, were really directed not against the law itself but against that misunderstanding and misuse of it for which we now have a convenient terminology. In this very difficult terrain Paul was pioneering.[41]

If Cranfield is right, as I believe he is, we should approach Sha'ul with the same pioneering spirit. We should understand *erga nomou* not as "works of law," but as "legalistic observance of particular *Torah* commands." Likewise, we should take *upo nomon* to mean not "under the law" but "in subjection to the system that results from perverting *Torah* into legalism." This is

---

39   C. E. B. Cranfield, "St. Paul and the Law," in *Scottish Journal of Theology* (1964), pp. 43-68.
40   Cranfield (*op. cit.* in footnote 6, above), volume 2, pp. 845-862.
41   *Ibid.*, p. 853.

how these phrases are rendered in the *Jewish New Testament*.

The expression "in subjection" is important because the context of *upo nomon* always conveys an element of oppressiveness. Sha'ul is very clear about this, as can be seen from 1 Corinthians 9:20, where, after saying that for those without *Torah* he became as one without *Torah*, he stressed that he was himself not without *Torah* but *ennomos Christou*, "en-lawed" or "en-*Torah*ed of Messiah." He used a different term, *ennomos* in place of *upo nomon*, to distinguish his oppression-free relationship with the *Torah*, now that he is united with the Messiah, from the sense of being burdened which he noticed in people (probably Gentiles![42]) who instead of happily "en-lawing" themselves to God's holy, just and good *Torah* subjected themselves to a legalistic perversion of it.

If the above renderings of *upo nomon* and *erga nomou* were used in the 20 passages where these phrases occur, I believe it would change Christian theology of *Torah* for the better.

c. Galatians 3:10-13 — Redeemed From The Curse Of The Law?

Galatians 3:10-13 presents a number of stumblingblocks in most translations. As an example, here is the New American Standard Bible's rendering, which strikes me as neither better nor worse than most:

> [10] For as many as are of the works of the Law are under a curse; for it is written, "Cursed is every one who does not abide by all things written in the book of the Law, to perform them." [11] Now that no one is justified by the Law before God is evident; for, "The righteous man shall live by faith." [12] However, the Law is not of faith; on the contrary, "He who practices them shall live by them." [13] Christ redeemed us from the curse of the Law, having become a curse for us —

---

42 For a discussion of why "those under law" are Gentiles, see notes to 1 Corinthians 9:20 in the *Jewish New Testament*.

for it is written, "Cursed is every one who hangs on a tree."

These verses appear as follows in the *Jewish New Testament*:

[10] For everyone who depends on legalistic observance of *Torah* commands [*erga nomou*] lives under a curse, since it is written, "Cursed is everyone who does not keep on doing everything written in the Scroll of the *Torah*." [Deuteronomy 27:26] [11] Now it is evident that no one comes to be declared righteous by God through legalism [*nomos*], since "The person who is righteous will attain life by trusting and being faithful." [Habakkuk 2:4] [12] Furthermore, legalism [*nomos*] is not based on trusting and being faithful, but on a misuse of the text that says, "Anyone who does these things will attain life through them." [Leviticus 18:5] [13] The Messiah redeemed us from the curse pronounced in the *Torah* [*nomos*] by becoming cursed on our behalf; for the *Tanakh* says, "Everyone who hangs from a stake comes under a curse." [Deuteronomy 21:22-23]

"The curse of the law" is not the curse of having to live within the framework of *Torah* for the *Torah* itself is good. Nor is it the curse of being required to obey the *Torah* but lacking the power to do so — this would be a kind of "Catch 22" unworthy of God, although there are theologies which teach that this is exactly the case. Rather, it is "the curse pronounced in the *Torah*" (v. 13; see v. 10) for disobeying it. Sha'ul's point is that that curse falls on people who are actually trying to *obey* the *Torah* if their efforts are grounded in legalism (vv. 11a, 12). For Sha'ul, a legalistic approach is already *dis*obedience; for the *Tanakh* itself requires genuine obedience to emerge from faith (v. 11b). There is not space here to prove that this is the case or to deal with other controversies raised by the above rendering of these four verses; my *Jewish New Testament* commentary addresses these matters.

*d.   Messianic Jews [Hebrews] 8:6 — The New Covenant Has
      Been Given as* Torah.

One of the most surprising discoveries I made in the course of
preparing the *Jewish New Testament* is that the New Covenant
itself has actually been given as *Torah* — as much as, and in
exactly the sense that, what Moses received on Mount Sinai
was given as *Torah*. The verse which hides this extremely well
kept secret is Messianic Jews [Hebrews] 8:6, which reads in a
typical translation,

> But as it is, Christ has obtained a ministry which is as
> much more excellent than the old as the covenant he
> mediates is better, since it is enacted on better promises.

The passage would seem poor ore for my mining efforts. But
upon examining the Greek text I noticed that the phrase "is
enacted on" renders the word *nenomothetêtai*, a compound of
our friend *nomos* ("law, *Torah*") with the common verb *tithêmi*
("to put, place"). If the subject matter of the Letter to a Group
of Messianic Jews were, say, Greek law, or the Roman Senate,
it would be appropriate to translate this word as "enacted,
established, legislated", that is, "put" or "placed as law".

But in the letter to these Messianic Jews, the word *nomos*,
which appears 14 times, always means *Torah* specifically, never
legislation in general. Moreover, the only other appearance of
nenomothetêtai in the New Testament is a few verses back, at
Messianic Jews 7:11, where it can only refer to the giving of the
Torah at Sinai (the related word *nomothesia*, "giving of the
Torah," at Romans 9:4 is equally unambiguous). Therefore the
Jewish New Testament renders Messianic Jews 8:6:

> But now the work Yeshua has been given to do is far
> superior to theirs, just as the covenant he mediates is
> better. For this covenant has been given as *Torah* on the
> basis of better promises.

So the New Covenant has been "given as *Torah*," which
implies that *Torah* still exists and is to be observed in the present

age — by all Jews and by all Gentiles, as we shall see. However, precisely what is demanded of "all Jews" and of "all Gentiles" is not quite so obvious. We will address this question in a limited way, but comprehensive treatment is beyond the scope of this book.

3. The Gospel With An Ended Law Is No Gospel At All.

The statement has been made (I'm not saying I agree) that of the three items mentioned earlier as most important on the Jewish theological agenda, Reform Jews focus mainly on "God," the Conservatives on "Israel," and the Orthodox on *"Torah."* Reform and secular Jews disagree with the Orthodox and Conservative over whether the *Torah* is binding forever, while Conservative Jews deny the exclusive claim of Orthodoxy to determine specific applications of what they agree is a *Torah* which binds. Nevertheless, although Orthodox Jews constitute only 15-20% of the Jewish population in Israel and less in the United States, their view of *Torah* as eternal has found a very deep place in the heart of the Jewish people; so that the non-Orthodox find themselves somewhat in the role of upstarts trying to dislodge a clever, experienced and self-confident ruler.

Now if Christianity comes into such an environment with the message that the *Torah* is no longer in force, the line of communication with Orthodox Judaism is simply cut. There is no longer anything to discuss. Moreover, if I am correct about the role of the Orthodox Jewish view of *Torah* in the Jewish mentality, then even the secular Jew "knows" at some level, whether correctly or not, that Orthodoxy is right. In fact there are secular Jews who, though not religious themselves, regard the Orthodox as the preservers of the Jewish nation.

Thus, if Christianity cannot address the issue of *Torah* properly and seriously, it has nothing to say to the Jewish people. Individual Jews may be won away to Christianity, across the wide gap between the Jewish people and the Church (look back at Figure 2E); but the central concern of Orthodox

Judaism itself is dismissed, perhaps with a casual and cavalier citation of Romans 6:14, "We're not under the law but under grace." In my opinion this shallow, sterile way of thinking has gone on too long in the Church, and it serves no purpose but the Adversary's!

Moreover, this way of thinking is not only shallow, but perverse! Yeshua said very plainly in the theme sentence of the Sermon on the Mount, "Do not think that I came to abolish the Law...; I did not come to abolish, but *plērôsai*," "to fill." We learned earlier[43] that Yeshua's "filling" here means making clear the full and proper sense of the *Torah*; and we pointed out that even if *pleroô* meant "fulfillment," it could not be twisted to mean "abolition," in contradiction to what he had said three words earlier. This seems so clear that it is hard for me to understand how Christian theology has even dared to propose the idea that the *Torah* is no more. I myself believe it came about because of anti-Jewish bias infused into the Gentile Church in its early centuries;[44] this bias is now so pervasive and difficult to root out that even Christians without any personal antisemitism whatever are unavoidably affected by it.

The remedy is to reassess the theology of *Torah*. I am convinced it will be found that the *Torah* continues in force. When I say this, I am not making a "concession to Judaism," as some Christian critics might suppose. Nor am I somehow expressing anti-*Torah* theology in hypocritical, deceptive and confusing pro-*Torah* language, an accusation I could expect from a few non-Messianic Jews. Rather, I am stating as clearly as I can what I believe the New Testament teaches. It will prove to be neither a concession nor a confusion, but a challenge — to both Jews and Christians.

For a key element of the New Covenant, both as promised

---

43   Section D-3 above.
44   It was the Adversary (Satan) who infused this anti-Jewish bias into the Church. He hates the Jews with unending fury because God chose to act in history through them. But Satan can enter only where there is no defense against him (Mattityahu [Matthew] 12:43-45).

by Jeremiah and as cited in the Letter To A Group of Messianic Jews ["To The Hebrews"], is that the *Torah* is written on people's hearts (Jeremiah 31:30-34, Messianic Jews 8:9-12). It takes unacceptable theological legerdemain to conclude that when God writes the *Torah* on hearts he changes it into something other than the *Torah!*

But if Messianic Jews and Gentile Christians acknowledge the ongoingness of the *Torah*, then the question arises, "Just what does the *Torah* require, now that Yeshua the Messiah has inaugurated the New Covenant? What is the New Covenant *halakhah*?[45] This is already a Jewish question, and, as we will see, an essential element of the Gospel.

For there is a tradition within Judaism which says that when the Messiah comes he will explain the difficult questions of *Torah*. Another tradition says he will change the *Torah*. Yeshua the Messiah has already come; some things he has explained — for example, in the Sermon on the Mount — and other things have been changed, as we learn later in the chapter. (When he comes the second time he may give more explanations and make more changes!) A Jew can cope with this kind of approach to *Torah*. And the Christian will just have to get used to it.

4. *New Covenant* Halakhot.

In fact, the New Testament does not leave us entirely in the dark

---

45 *Halakhah* means, literally, "way of walking"; but, depending on the context, it can convey either the broad sense, "way of living, according to the *Torah*," or the narrow sense, "the rule to be followed" in a particular situation. In Jewish discourse when one speaks of "the *halakhah*," one is bringing to mind the whole framework of Jewish life as seen from a particular viewpoint. Sometimes the intent is to know what is permitted and what is forbidden by Jewish law; however, just as often the concern in not "legal" but simply related to finding out what the customs are, and perhaps why they are that way. The phrase "the *halakhah*" connotes Jewish peoplehood spanning centuries and expressing itself through ordinary Jews consulting with their rabbis in order to learn more about how God wants them to live.

on the question of what is the New Covenant *halakhah*. On the contrary, the New Testament actually states a number of *diney-torah* (specific judgments as to how to apply the *Torah*) or *halakhot* (applications of Law), and these are generally arrived at by thoroughly rabbinic ways of thinking. Here are five examples:

a. Yochanan [John] 7:22-23.

In this passage Yeshua presents a *din-torah* that the *mitzvah* of healing takes precedence over that of refraining from work on *Shabbat*. In making this decision as to which of two conflicting laws holds in a particular situation, he was doing much the same thing as did the rabbis who developed the Oral *Torah*. In fact, Yeshua referred in this passage to a well-known such decision which can be found in the Talmud, tractate *Shabbat*, pages 128a ff.

The rabbis were confronted with the conflict between the law against working on *Shabbat* and the commandment that a man should circumcise his son on the eighth day of his life. The conflict arises from the fact that cutting and carrying the tools needed to perform a *b'rit-milah* through a public domain are kinds of work forbidden by the rabbis on *Shabbat*. They decided that if the eighth day falls on *Shabbat*, one does the necessary work and circumcises the boy; but if the circumcision must take place after the eighth day, say, for health reasons, it may not be done on *Shabbat* in violation of the work prohibitions; one waits till a weekday.

Yeshua in defending his ruling used what Judaism calls a *kal v'homer* ("light and heavy") argument, known in philosophy as reasoning *a fortiori* ("from greater strength"). Its essence is the expressed or implied phrase "how much more...!" Yochanan [John] 7:23 says, in effect, "You permit breaking *Shabbat* in order to observe the *mitzvah* of circumcision; how much more important it is to heal a person's whole body, so you should permit breaking *Shabbat* for that too!"

b. Galatians 2:11-14.

Sha'ul pronounced an important *halakhah* at Galatians 2:11-14. It too is a decision as to how to proceed when two valid principles conflict, but in this case the conflict was between an Old Testament command and a New Covenant necessity. His conclusion was not, as some suppose, that the Jewish dietary laws no longer apply, but that Jewish believers' observance of *kashrut* must not be allowed to impede their fellowship with Gentile believers. Communion in the Messiah is more important than eating *kosher*. But when a Jewish believer's eating *kosher* does not break such fellowship, then nothing in Galatians 2:11-14 can be construed to imply that the Jewish dietary laws should not be observed.

c. Mark 7:1-20.

While on the subject of *kashrut* we will look at two other passages commonly cited to prove its abolition and show that this is not their purpose. Mark 7:1-20 is concerned not with *kashrut* but with ritual washing before meals *(n'tilat-yadayim)*, a practice observed in traditional Judaism today.[46] Therefore when Yeshua "declared all foods clean"[47] he was not declaring *treif* foods *kosher*, but saying that *kosher* food is not rendered ritually unclean when hands not ritually washed touch it. Although in our age it is hard for anyone not an Orthodox Jew to think intelligently about ritual impurity, its importance in Yeshua's time can be roughly measured by the fact that one of the six major divisions of the Talmud (*Tohorot*, "Purities") is almost entirely devoted to this subject.

However, the important *halakhah* for us to note has nothing to do with eating. In this passage Yeshua does not give zero weight to the "tradition of the elders," as do many Christians. Rather, what he does insist on is that human traditions should not be used to "make null and void the word

---

46   See Mark 7:2-5.
47   Mark 7:19.

of God." This is a key *halakhic* ruling by the Messiah himself
which can guide us in creating New Testament *halakhah* today.
It says that we must keep our priorities straight: only God's
word commands absolute obedience. Our *halakhot* may be
useful, suggestive, edifying, valuable as guidance, but they are
still only "tradition of men," hence fallible and less important.
The Messiah's *halakhah* contrasts with the prevailing view in
Orthodox Judaism, which, being descended directly from the
Pharisaic position Yeshua criticized, can regard violation of a
rabbinic ruling as more severe than violation of a biblical
precept.

d. Acts 10:9-17, 28.

Kefa [Peter] had a vision in which three times he saw *treif*
animals being lowered from heaven in a sheet and heard a voice
telling him to "kill and eat." Unlike those interpreters who
instantly assume the passage teaches that Jews need not eat
kosher food any more, Kefa spent some time "puzzling over the
meaning of the vision." Only when he arrived at Cornelius'
home did he get the pieces of the puzzle put together, so that he
could state, "God has shown me not to call any *person*
unclean." The vision was about people, not food. It did not
teach Kefa, who had always eaten *kosher*, to change his eating
habits, but to accept Gentiles equally with Jews as candidates
for salvation.

For it must be remembered that the sheet lowered from
heaven contained all kinds of animals, wild beasts, reptiles and
birds; yet I know of no Bible interpreters who insist that eagles,
vultures, owls, bats, weasels, mice, lizards, crocodiles, chame-
leons, snakes, spiders and bugs must now be considered edible.
God specifies in Leviticus 11 what Jews are to regard as "food."
Even if there were a secondary message in this vision about
eating, it would not totally overthrow the dietary laws but
would state the same rule we found above in Galatians 2:11-14,

that preserving fellowship between Jewish and Gentile believers supersedes observance of *kashrut*.[48]

e. *Acts 15 And The* Torah.

In Acts 15, the Jerusalem Council, a kind of Messianic *Sanhedrin*, was convened to determine under what conditions Gentile believers were to be accepted into the Messianic Community (that is, into the Church). It was decided that they need not convert to Judaism but should initially observe four *halakhot* — "to abstain from things polluted by idols, from fornication, from what is strangled and from blood."[49]

This teaches us that the elements of *Torah* which apply to Gentiles under the New Covenant are not the same as those which apply to Jews. (The Jerusalem Council made no change whatever in the *Torah* as it applies to Jews, so that a number of years later there could still be in Jerusalem "tens of thousands" of Messianic Jews who were "zealots for the *Torah*."[50]) It should not surprise us if New Covenant *Torah* specifies different commandments for Jews and Gentiles. First, the Five Books of Moses have commands which apply to some groups and not others — to the king but not to his subjects, to *cohanim* ("priests") but not to other Jews, to men but not women. Second, the New Testament too has different commands for different categories of people, for example, men and women, husbands and wives, parents and children, slaves and masters, leaders and followers, widows.[51]

However, Acts 15 also teaches that although Gentiles were *required* to observe only four laws upon entering the Messianic Community, they were *permitted* to learn as much about

---

48   For more on this subject, see my notes on Galatians 2:11-14 in the *Jewish New Testament*.
49   Acts 15:20.
50   Acts 21:20, *Jewish New Testament*.
51   See 1 Corinthians 11:2-16, 14:34-36; Ephesians 5:22-6:9; Colossians 3:18-4:1; 1 Timothy 3:1-13, 5:3-16; Messianic Jews 13:7, 17; 1 Kefa [1 Peter] 3:1-7.

Judaism as they wished [52] and presumably to observe as many
Jewish laws and customs as they wished. The only proviso
added in the New Covenant (in Galatians) is that Gentiles
should not suppose that their self-Judaizing will earn them
"salvation points" with God.

Moreover, it should not be thought that the only requirement the New Covenant makes of Gentiles is to obey these four
commands. On the contrary, there are hundreds of commands
in the New Testament meant as much for Gentiles as for Jews.
Nor should it be thought that the New Covenant does away
with moral, civil, ceremonial or any other category of law.
There are New Testament commands for Jews and Gentiles in
all of these categories. To give but a few examples, Romans
13:1-7 and Acts 5:29 touch on civil obedience and disobedience,
Mattityahu [Matthew] 28:19 and 1 Corinthians 11:17-34 deal
with matters of ceremony, 1 Corinthians 5:1-6:7, 14:26-40, 2
Corinthians 2:5-11 and Matthew 18:15-17 deal with order in the
Messianic Community, and there are so many moral, ethical
and spiritual commands that there is no need to cite them (1050
commands of all kinds, according to one enumeration)[53].

We conclude that under the New Covenant the *Torah*
remains in force and is as much for Gentiles as for Jews,
although the specific requirements for Gentiles differ from
those for Jews.

5. *New Covenant* Halakhah

It's easy for many Gentile Christians to agree with the abstract
statement that the *Torah* is still in force under the New
Covenant, for they are unlikely to have a sense of how to draw
out its implications. But a Jew who agrees should immediately
wonder how the *Torah* is applied. What is the *halakhah* under

---

52   Acts 15:21.
53   Finnis Jennings Dake, *Dake's Annotated Reference Bible* (Lawrence-
     ville, Georgia: Dake Bible Sales, Inc., 1961), New Testament, pp.
     313-316.

the New Covenant? What ought to be done, and what ought not to be done in particular situations? Should one refrain from lighting fires or from driving on *Shabbat*? Should a man wear a *kippah* (head covering) in a congregational meeting? Should he wear *tzitziyot* (tassels on the corners of his garment, per Numbers 15:37-41)? Should the leader of a Messianic Jewish congregation be called a rabbi? May a Messianic Gentile be called up to read from the *Torah* scroll in a Messianic synagogue? May a Gentile Christian convert to Judiasm? and if so, under what auspices? How should Messianic Jews relate to the State of Israel? Should Messianic Jews immigrate to Israel? Is there *halakhah* concerning when a Messianic Jew might marry a Gentile Christian? Should a Messianic Jew light *Shabbat* candles? and if he does, should he recite the traditional *b'rakhah* (benediction), which states that God commanded the lighting of candles on *Shabbat*? (There is no such command in the Bible.) To what extent may or should Gentile members of Messianic Jewish congregations imitate or take on Jewish practices? Etcetera.

Should the creation of New Covenant *halakhah* follow the pattern of (non-Messianic) Judaism? One can imagine creating a body of New Testament case law much like the Talmud, the Codes and the Responsa. It would take into consideration Jewish *halakhah*, which has, after all, dealt with nearly every sector of human existence; yet everything would have to be reexamined in the light of the New Testament. It would be created by both Jewish and Gentile believers, with the prime text on which to base such a procedure being Mattityahu [Matthew]18:18-20:

> "Yes! I tell you [disciples in leadership] that whatever you bind [that is, prohibit] on earth will be bound in heaven, and whatever you loose [permit] on earth will be loosed in heaven. To repeat, I tell you that if two of you here on earth agree about anything people ask, it will be for them from my Father in heaven. For

wherever two or three are assembled in my name, I am there with them."[54]

The last sentence is commonly regarded as assurance that Yeshua is present with believers when they pray. That is true, but not on the basis of this verse. Yeshua here is speaking to people who have authority to regulate Messianic communal life (see the preceding three verses). He says that they — and presumably subsequent leaders — have the right to establish *halakhah*, because the terms "bind" and "loose" were used in first-century Judaism to mean "prohibit" and "permit." Yeshua is teaching that when an issue is brought formally to a panel of two or three Messianic Community leaders, and they render a halakhic decision here on earth, they can be assured that the authority of God stands behind them.

But what good would such a body of *halakhah* do? Who would observe it? Who needs it? Does anyone even want it? Are we not guided in all things by the Holy Spirit? Do we require a set of rules or guidelines?

Well — there you have a start to the debate. I will not presume to be able to finish it, although my longer book, *Messianic Jewish Manifesto*, carries the discussion a few stages further. But even as little as has been presented here sheds a gleam of light on the Jewish elements of *Torah* that are present in the Gospel. I fervently hope that the Church will never again be able to brush them aside with the slogan, "Free from the Law!" So far as achieving the goal of the Great Commission is concerned, free-from-the-law is head-in-the-sand.

---

54   Mattityahu [Matthew] 18:18-20, *Jewish New Testament*.

CHAPTER III

PRESUPPOSITIONS TO RESTORING THE JEWISHNESS OF THE GOSPEL

In the Introduction I wrote that I assume my readers will agree to the following three points, which are not themselves part of restoring Jewishness to the Gospel but are presupposed by it: (1) Christianity is Jewish, (2) Antisemitism is un-Christian, and (3) refusing or neglecting to evangelize Jews is antisemitic. The time has come to discuss these matters, since some readers will not have agreed and need to be convinced. We will conclude by considering what Sha'ul [Paul] meant when he wrote in Romans 1:16 that the Gospel is "for the Jew first."

A. Christianity is Jewish.

Edith Schaeffer, wife of the late Francis Schaeffer, wrote a book with the title, *Christianity is Jewish.*[1] Her point, and mine too, is that Christianity, no matter how un-Jewish some of its current forms of expression may be, has its roots in Judaism and in the Jewish people.

The facts are simply not a matter of debate. For years all the disciples of Yeshua were Jewish. The New Testament was entirely written by Jews (Luke being, in all likelihood, a Jewish proselyte). The very concept of a Messiah is nothing but Jewish. Finally, Yeshua himself was Jewish — was then and apparently

---

1   Edith Schaeffer, *Christianity is Jewish* (Wheaton, Illinois: Tyndale House Publishers, Inc., 1975).

is still, since nowhere does Scripture say or suggest that he has ceased to be a Jew. It was Jews who brought the Gospel to Gentiles. Sha'ul, the chief emissary to the Gentiles was an observant Jew all his life. Indeed the main issue in the early Church was whether without undergoing complete conversion to Judaism a Gentile could be a Christian at all. The Messiah's vicarious atonement is rooted in the Jewish sacrificial system; the Lord's Supper is rooted in the Jewish Passover traditions; baptism is a Jewish practice; and indeed the entire New Testament is built on the Hebrew Bible, with its prophecies and its promise of a New Covenant, so that the New testament without the Old is as impossible as the second floor of a house without the first.

Moreover, much of what is written in the New Testament is incomprehehsible apart from Judaism. In the previous chapter's discussion of Mattityahu [Matthew] 18:18-20 we already gave one example of this,[2] but here is another. Yeshua tells us in the Sermon on the Mount, 'If thine eye be evil, thy whole body shall be full of darkness.'[3] What is an evil eye? Someone not knowing the Jewish background might suppose he was talking about casting spells. But in Hebrew, having an *'ayin ra'ah*, an "evil eye," means being stingy; while having an *'ayin tovah*, a "good eye," means being generous. Yeshua is warning against lack of generosity and nothing else. Moreover, this fits the context perfectly: "Where your treasure is, there will your heart be also. ... You cannot serve both God and money."[4]

The Jewishness of Christian faith is clear throughout the New Testament, but Sha'ul makes it explicit in the book of Romans. He writes, "In the first place, the Jews were entrusted with the very words of God,"[5] meaning the Hebrew Bible, and then expands on the theme, adding that the people of Israel

---

2   Chapter II, Section F-5.
3   Mattityahu [Matthew] 6:23.
4   Mattityahu [Matthew] 6:21, 24.
5   Romans 3:2.

were made God's children, the *Sh'khinah* [God's glory manifested] has been with them, the covenants are theirs, likewise the giving of the *Torah*, the Temple service and the promises; the Patriarchs are theirs; and from them, as far as his physical descent is concerned, came the Messiah. ...[6]

Thus although the Gospel message is for Jew and Gentile equally, the context of Messianic faith is Jewish. Even if one were to accept the false premise of Replacement Theology that the Jews are no longer God's people, this would not change the fact that Christianity is Jewish. To try to understand it differently can only distort God's message.

But Christianity is Jewish in yet another sense, namely, that it is in principle best assimilated by Jews. This is Sha'ul's very point in the quoted passages of Romans; his object is to show that the Gospel is "for the Jew *especially*" — as we will see.

B. Antisemitism Is Un-Christian.

Antisemitism is incompatible with biblical faith. At Zechariah 2:8 God says, "He who touches you" — the Jewish people — "touches the apple of my eye," that is, the pupil, the most sensitive and useful part. At Genesis 12:3 God assures Abraham, the father of the Jewish people, "I will bless those who bless you and curse him who curses you."

Nevertheless both individuals and the Church as an institution have taught antisemitic doctrines and committed antisemitic acts in the name of Christ. Moreover, although some of these individuals were Christians in name only, displaying no evidence of genuine faith, others were people who according to any criterion except that of the antisemitism itself really were Christians — such as Augustine and Martin Luther. In fact, even though he inaugurated the Protestant Reformation one can seriously wonder, in the light of the standard set by Genesis

---

6   Romans 9:4-5.

12:3, if the man who filled his tract, "On the Jews and their Lies,"[7] with imprecations against Abraham's descendants was saved.

I think it is appropriate for Gentile Christians and Messianic Jews to take responsibility for these things, to be humble about them, to take the stance of personally acknowledging the Church's guilt before Jews without necessarily expecting to be forgiven by them.

But more importantly, it must be understood by all that any thoughts, words or deeds which damage Jewish individuals or the Jewish people as a whole merely because they are Jews violates everything Christian and must be regarded as sin.

---

7   Martin Luther, "On The Jews And Their Lies" (1543), translated by
     Martin H. Bertram, edited by Franklin Sherman: Volume 47, pp.
     121-306 of Jaroslav Pelikan and Helmut T. Lehmann, *Luther's
     Works* (Philadelphia: Fortress Press and St. Louis: Concordia Pub-
     lishing House, 1962-1974). The following is selected from pp.
     268-278:

     What shall we Christians do with this rejected and
     condemned people, the Jews? ... I shall give you my
     sincere advice: First, to set fire to their synagogues ... in
     honor of our Lord and of Christendom, so that God might
     see that we are Christians. ... I advise that their houses
     also be razed and destroyed. ... I advise that their
     prayerbooks and Talmudic writings ... be taken from
     them. ... I advise that their rabbis be forbidden to teach
     henceforth on pain of loss of life and limb. ... [W]e will
     believe that our Lord Jesus Christ is truthful when he
     declares of the Jews who did not accept but crucified him,
     "You are a brood of vipers and children of the devil...." I
     have read and heard many stories about the Jews which
     agree with this judgment of Christ, namely, how they have
     poisoned wells, made assassinations, kidnapped children.
     ... I have heard that one Jew sent another Jew, and this by
     means of a Christian, a pot of blood, together with a barrel
     of wine, in which when drunk empty, a dead Jew was
     found. ...

     It does not make edifying reading. Further analysis is contained in
     my unpublished paper, "Luther's View Of The Jews: A Lesson For
     Our Time," 1974.

Finally, there are unconscious forms of antisemitism — a rereading of this book will point at many of them.[8] Well-meaning Christians who neither dislike nor wish to offend Jews nevertheless absorb anti-Jewish attitudes from a culture steeped in centuries of anti-Jewish teaching. Replacing anti-Jewish interpretations of the New Testament with interpretations based on its Jewish background may be the one effective way of dealing with this phenomenon.

C. Refusing Or Neglecting To Evangelize Jews Is Antisemitic.

Only bigots and boors would dispute the first two points in this chapter. But there are many who call themselves Christians who would disagree with this third point, who would insist that what is proper and appropriate is *not* to bring the Gospel to Jewish people, either as individuals or as a people. Others do not actually refuse to evangelize Jews on principle, but simply neglect to do so, considering it a relatively low priority in their Christian lives.

So in this section we must establish that evangelism of Jews should be high-priority for every Christian.

1. Benign Neglect Of The Jews Is Antisemitic.

There are Christians who justify their neglect of Jewish evangelism with remarks such as, "I don't know any Jews,;" "I've never thought about Judaism;" "God hasn't called me to concern myself with Jews."

All are unsatisfactory excuses, because Scripture does not allow the option of overlooking the Jews. Zechariah 1:15 is a very interesting verse. God tells the prophet, "I am highly displeased with the *goyim*" — the Hebrew word can mean Gentiles, pagans, or nations — "who are at ease; for I was only a

---

8   See also my *Messianic Jewish Manifesto* (*op. cit.* in Chapter I, footnote 3), Chapter III, Section E-4.

little displeased, but they helped forward the affliction." How did the Gentiles help "forward the affliction" of the Jews? By being "at ease" — indifferent, not caring, ignoring the situation. Edmund Burke noted that the world's evil can be laid at the feet of good men who sit back and do nothing. Yeshua himself said, "Those who are not with me are against me, and those who do not gather with me are scattering."[9] There is no middle position, no *tertium quid*. Everyone must take a stand; taking no stand is taking a stand against by default.

If indifference to the Jewish people counts as opposition and is wrong, then what is right? What is right is to bring the Gospel to the Jewish people in a way that takes seriously their position as the people of God, whose gift and calling, Sha'ul wrote, are irrevocable. Or, to put it differently, what is right is to be a channel for God's love to the Jews.

2. Purposeful Neglect, Justified By History, Is Antisemitic.

But there are also people who call themselves Christians who not only neglect Jews and refuse to evangelize them, but do so on purpose and believe that they are right.

Some are simply afraid of being rejected, since it is well known that many Jewish people are not open to considering the claims of Yeshua and the New Testament. If that is their only reason, they can be encouraged to drop their fear, pray that God will bless their efforts, and then obey the Great Commission by reaching out to the Jews with the offer of God's love and forgiveness through the Messiah.

Others feel they should respect the sensibilities of Jewish people who say they do not want to hear about Yeshua. For them the remedy is to give Scripture heavier weight than their feelings and to renew their efforts — tactfully, sensitively, as the

---

9   Luke 11:23.

Lord leads — at communicating the truth of the Gospel to Jews.

However, others do not rely on emotions but attempt to rationalize steering clear of Jewish evangelism by objective facts. A common justification for not evangelizing Jews arises from the Holocaust. Six million Jews died at the hands of the Nazis. During Hitler's twelve-year rule the state churches were notoriously silent and weak in the face of visible evil; moreover, mainstream Christian theology, if not actually antisemitic, was sufficiently cold toward Jews and Judaism to allow virulent antisemitism to express itself unchecked. Many well-meaning Christians ask how, in the face of such sin by the Church, do we dare tell Jews they should believe in Jesus?

The answer is twofold. On the one hand, the answer to the question, "How?" is: "Humbly." A Christian should be willing to shoulder the burden of the Church in respect to the Jews. He should not say, "The bad Christian theology was done by liberals, and they weren't real Christians. The state churches were not run by real Christians." Instead, he should admit, "It is possible that people who are my brothers in Christ committed horrors against Jews. I don't know for certain that they really are my brothers, but I will not massage my own conscience by denying the possibility categorically."

Moreover, his stance toward Jews in regard to the Holocaust should be one of seeking forgiveness without expecting it. He should acknowledge that the Church sinned. And he should ask forgiveness. But why should a Jew grant it? What has the Church done to earn the Jewish people's forgiveness? An element in forgiveness is restitution. How can the Church, or anyone, make restitution for the death of six million people? Ultimately, the answer is that only God can make restitution. The Holocaust is too horrible to allow that any human act or combination of human acts could pay for it. Only God, in his miraculous way, through the healing that Yeshua the Messiah brings, can restore the hearts of the living to the point to where they can forgive. No Christian has a right to expect Jewish forgiveness for the Holocaust, and in fact he will probably not get such forgiveness from Jews whose hearts have not been healed by Yeshua the Messiah.

Nevertheless, a Christian should bring the Gospel to the Jews. Why? Because it is true, and because it is necessary — without Yeshua Jewish people, like Gentile people, are destined for eternal destruction; moreover, without Yeshua, the true Messiah of the Jewish people, the Jewish people will not achieve its own glorious goals promised by Scripture. *Not to preach the Gospel to Jews is the worst antisemitic act of all.* Therefore, in spite of the Holocaust — and the Inquisition, and the pogroms, and all the other horrors — Christians must take up the Gospel and bring it to Jews. For without Yeshua, the Jewish people (and other peoples), individually and collectively, have no hope.

3. *Purposeful Neglect, Justified By Theology, Is Antisemitic*

Another way in which Christians who will not evangelize Jews justify themselves is through two-covenant theology. This says that Jesus brought the covenant through which Gentiles emerge from paganism to know the one true God; but that Jews already have the covenant through Moses, so that they do not need Yeshua the Messiah — in fact, it is both a diversion and an insult to tell Jews about him.

The first objection to this is simply a matter of logic. If Yeshua is not the Messiah of the Jews, then he is nobody's Messiah, and Gentiles don't need him either.

But for anyone who accepts the New Testament as God-given, one verse is enough to blow two-covenant theology out of the arena, Yochanan [John] 14:6: "Yeshua said, 'I am the way and the truth and the life; no one comes to the father except through me.'" This verse teaches that *no one* — neither Jew nor Gentile — comes to the Father except through Yeshua the Messiah. If that weren't sufficient, there is also Acts 4:12, where

Kefa [Peter] says of Yeshua, "There is salvation in no one else! For there is no other name under heaven given to mankind by whom we must be saved!" — no other name but Yeshua given to mankind for salvation, not to Gentiles and not to Jews.

It is understandable that two-covenant theology began not in Christianity but in Judaism, since it provides a Jewish defense against the Gospel. The Rambam ("Rambam" is an acronym for Rabbi Moshe ben-Maimon, known as Maimonides, 1135-1204), functioning in an environment wherein Christendom controlled the state and all major institutions, developed the theory that Christianity was right for Gentiles, since it enabled them to stop worshipping idols and to worship instead the God of Abraham, Isaac and Jacob. Their worship was imperfect because it was mixed with worshipping a man as well as God; but imperfect worship of God was better than idolatry. This was a relatively sanguine view of Christianity, compared with Jewish opinions which regarded Christianity itself as idolatry.

In the early twentieth century this approach was picked up by the Jewish philosopher Franz Rosenzweig (1886-1929), who had seriously considered converting to Christianity but was won back to Judaism by experiencing the beauty and depth of a *Yom Kippur* synagogue service. In his book *The Star Of Redemption* he expressed the two-covenant theory in modern theological language. Yeshua is truly the Messiah for the Gentiles, he argued, even if he isn't for the Jews. Rosenzweig even came up with an answer to Yochanan [John] 14:6. Yes, Jesus is the way, the truth and the life for Gentiles, and no one comes to the Father except through him. But Jews are *already* with the Father, because of the Mosaic and Abrahamic covenants; so they don't need to *come* to him. Reinhold Niebuhr, the theologian, and James Parkes, the historian who wrote extensively about the relationship between the Church and the Synagogue, were among those who proposed the two-covenant theory within a Christian thought-framework. They were well-meaning, but they missed the essential point that according to the New Testament (*e.g.*, Ephesians 2:11-16), Jews and Christians can be reconciled with God and with each other only when both accept Yeshua as Messiah, Savior and Lord.

For Yochanan 14:6 cannot be so easily disposed of. Yeshua was speaking to Jews when he said those words; moreover, when he spoke them, the Gospel had been presented only to Israel, so that there is no reason to suppose he was referring to Gentiles. Likewise, Mark tells us that only hours later his answer to the high priest's question, "Are you the *Mashiach, Ben-HaM'vorakh* [the Messiah, the Son of the Blessed One]?" was umistakable: "I AM." Then, to make his answer crystal clear, he cited two verses from the *Tanakh* with Messianic overtones, Psalm 110:1 and Daniel 7:13: "Moreover, you will see 'the Son of Man' 'sitting at the right hand of *HaG'vurah*' ['the Power,' i.e., God] and 'coming on the clouds of heaven.'"[10] The very concept of a Messiah is Jewish, not Gentile. All four Gospels depict him coming from Jews, to Jews and for Jews (while not excluding others). The two-covenant theory is fantasy and wish, not truth and reality.

Yeshua himself longed to be accepted by the Jewish people as who he is. But he did not force people to receive him, nor would he allow others to use force to obtain for him what was his by right.[11] Rather, he wept, "Jerusalem! Jerusalem! ... How often I wanted to gather your children, just as a hen gathers her chickens under her wings, but you refused! ... For I tell you, from now on, you will not see me again until you say, 'Blessed is he who comes in the name of *Adonai.*'"[12]

In conclusion, Yeshua is the Messiah of both Jews and Gentiles. There is one New Covenant, made "with the house of Israel and the house of Judah," (Jeremiah 31:30-34) for both Jews and Gentiles. Jews need Yeshua and the New Covenant as much as Gentiles. It is up to Gentile Christians and Messianic

---

10   Mark 14:61-62, *Jewish New Testament.*
11   Yochanan [John] 6:15.
12   Mattityahu [Matthew] 23:37, 39, *Jewish New Testament.*

Jews to make this known to unsaved Jews as well as unsaved Gentiles, not to find excuses for disobeying the Great Commission.

4. Romans 1:16 — The Gospel Is "For The Jew Especially."

Romans 1:16 (in the *Jewish New Testament* version) says,

> For I am not ashamed of the Good News, since it is God's powerful means of bringing salvation to everyone who keeps on trusting, to the Jew especially, but equally to the Gentile.

This rendering brings out the meaning of the phrase usually translated, "to the Jew first." Mitch Glaser, of Jews for Jesus, in his 1984 Covenant Theological Seminary lecture trenchantly entitled, "To The Jew First: The Starting Point For The Great Commission,"[13] presented three options for understanding this phrase. He concluded that it does not refer only to "historical priority," to the fact that historically the Gospel was presented first to Jews and only later to Gentiles, although this is true.

Nor does it refer only to "covenant priority," the idea that — as John Murray put it in his commentary on Romans — "salvation through faith has primary relevance to the Jew ... aris[ing] from the fact that [he] had been chosen by God to be the recipient of the promise of the Gospel and that to him were committed the oracles of God" — although this too is true.

Rather, "to the Jew first" means that there is a "present priority" in bringing the Gospel to Jews, and the Church should acknowledge it. This does not necessarily mean that every single believer should seek out the Jews in the community and witness to them before telling any Gentiles about Jesus —

---

13 Mitch Glaser, "To The Jew First: The Starting Point For The Great Commission," lecture presented at Covenant Theological Seminary, 1984. Manuscript available through Jews for Jesus, San Francisco, California.

although that is exactly what Sha'ul did throughout the book of Acts. As Mitch Glaser puts it, believers today should have

> a priority of Gospel concern for the Jewish people. . . . Perhaps the most lucid explanation of the Present Priority view of Romans 1:16 can be found in the statement of the Lausanne Consultation on Jewish Evangelism, Occasional Papers No. 7:
>
> > There is, therefore, a great responsibility laid upon the church to share Christ with the Jewish people. This is not to imply that Jewish evangelism is more important in the sight of God, or that those involved in Jewish evangelism have a higher calling. We observe that the practical application of the scriptural priority is difficult to understand and apply. We do not suggest that there should be a radical application of "to the Jew first" in calling on all the evangelists, missionaries, and Christians to seek out the Jews within their sphere of witness before speaking to non-Jews! Yet we do call the church to restore ministry among this covenanted people of God to its biblical place in the strategy of world evangelization.[14]

Christians pray in the Lord's Prayer, "Thy kingdom come, thy will be done on earth as it is in heaven." Jews pray in the *Kaddish*, "May he establish his kingdom in your lifetime and in your days, and within the life of the whole house of Israel, speedily and soon." 2 Kefa [2 Peter] 3:12 says believers in Yeshua should work to hasten the coming of the Day of God. Could it be that one reason for the "present priority" of preaching the Gospel "to the Jew especially" is that neglecting Jewish evangelism delays the coming of the Kingdom of God on earth?

---

14   *Ibid.*

CHAPTER IV

BLESSINGS

Why restore the Jewishness of the Gospel? In order to bless both the Church and the Jewish people.

A. How Will The Church Be Blessed?

How will the Church be blessed? We spoke already of Genesis 12:3, in which God tells Abraham, "I will bless those who bless my people." That is a blessing Christians can experience right now. Any blessing, either spiritual or material (see Romans 15:27) to the Jewish people will bring return blessings to the Church. "Cast your bread on the waters, for you will find it after many days."[1]

But there is a further blessing in store for the Church. Sha'ul [Paul] tells Gentile Christians concerning the Jewish people:

> For if their being cast aside means reconciliation for the
> world, what will their acceptance mean? It will be life
> from the dead![2]

It will be life from the dead both for Jews and for Christians. This is a powerful motive for successfully evangelizing the Jewish people. I emphasize "successfully," because Sha'ul here does not promise an "A" for effort. It is only when the Jews are actually "accepted" that "life from the dead" will come. And

---

1   Ecclesiastes 11:1.
2   Romans 11:15.

this "life from the dead" will not be merely what some Christians understand by "revival" — having a bit more energy and feeling good — but the Resurrection itself! The Resurrection will take place only when "all Israel shall be saved."

B. How Will The Jewish People Be Blessed?

How will the Jewish people be blessed? By being able to realize its age-old goal of being a light to the nations, and also by receiving the deliverance for which it has waited so long. The deliverance will be both individual and corporate, as we have seen.

How will these blessings come to the Jewish people? From God, of course. But not directly! Rather, they will come through the Church, and specifically through Gentile Christians[3] when they finally make Jews jealous![4]

Have Jews reason to be jealous of the Church now? A Jewish bumper sticker from some years ago said it all. In the "Key '73" evangelistic campaign Christians put stickers on their car bumpers with the slogan, "I found it," hoping to provoke at least interest, if not jealousy. Jews answered with stickers that said, "We never lost it."

Three things here: First, Jewish people understood well what the "it" was that the bumper sticker people had "found," namely, a relationship with God through Jesus. In effect proclaiming two-covenant theology to the world, their bumper stickers said that they already had a relationship with God and therefore didn't need Jesus; moreover, by implication they questioned the Christian theology that supposes people go out

---

3   Romans 11:30-32, quoted below.
4   Romans 10:19; 11:11, 14.

of relationship with God, so that they need to be saved.[5]

Secondly, the stickers poked fun at the very idea that as serious a matter as being related to the living God could be dealt with so offhandedly. You want to talk about ultimate matters of universal significance with slogans on bumper stickers? You found it? "It"? We should be jealous? You've got to be kidding!

Thirdly, the sticker says a lot about the difference between Judaism and Christianity as currently purveyed: *I*, all by myself in my little warm cocoon, found it; *WE*, the Jewish people, the people of God, never lost it. Corporate mentality — unfortunately Christianity, especially in most of its Protestant manifestations, lost it!

How will Christianity overcome its handicap? One way![6] By making Jewish people truly jealous. And how will Christians accomplish that? By showing God's mercy to Jewish people. This is what Sha'ul prescribes to Gentile Christians at the end of Romans 9-11:

> Just as you yourselves were disobedient to God before but have received mercy now because of Israel's disobedience; so also Israel has been disobedient now, so that by your showing them the same mercy that God has shown you, they too may now receive God's mercy. For God has shut up all mankind together in disobedience, in order that he might show mercy to all.[7]

Some suppose this passage says only that God will show Jews the same mercy he has shown Gentiles. This is true, but it misses the point. After severely warning Gentile Christians in Romans 11:17-24 not to boast against the cut-off branches (unsaved Jews), Sha'ul concluded his exhortation by counseling them to do something very different, to show them mercy. It will indeed

---

5   On this see Abba Hillel Silver, *Where Judaism Differed* (New York: The Macmillan Company, 1956), Chapter 10, entitled "That Men Need To Be Saved."

6   "One way!" was another "Key '73" slogan.

7   Romans 11:30-32, *Jewish New Testament*.

be the mercy which God has given them that they will channel to Jews. But Sha'ul is not calling for watching passively to see how God will show his mercy to Jews. Rather he adjures Gentile Christians to show mercy actively to Jews right now. God calls for active participation in his salvation program. This is the one thing that can melt hearts and make unsaved Jews jealous of Christians. Nothing else will! Too bad so few have tried it!

This remarkable plan of God's causes Sha'ul so to marvel that he breaks into song at the end of Romans 11, a song so joyous and profound that there is nothing to match it in the entire New Testament — and with it I close:

> O the depth of the riches
>   and the wisdom and knowledge of God!
> How inscrutable are his judgments!
>   How unsearchable are his ways!
>
> For from him and through him
>   and to him are all things.
> To him be the glory forever!
>   *Amen.*[8]

---

8   Romans 11:33, 36, *Jewish New Testament.*

GLOSSARY OF HEBREW
WORDS AND NAMES

Hebrew vowels and diphthongs are pronounced like those italicized in the following words: f*a*ther, *ai*sle, b*e*d, n*eig*hbor, *i*nvest (usually when not accented) or mar*i*ne (usually when accented), *o*bey, r*u*le; "ch" is pronounced as in Johann Sebastian Ba*ch*, and so is "kh"; "g" is always hard (*g*ive); other consonants are more or less as in English. Accented syllables are printed in **boldface**. Israeli pronunciation is shown generally; "Ashk" indicates certain Ashkenazic (German and eastern European) pronunciations common in English-speaking countries.

A·do·**nai** — my Lord, Lord of all; spoken by Jewish people instead of God's personal name Y-H-V-H ("Jehovah").

A·**men** — so be it; yes, indeed.

Av·ra·**ham** — Abraham.

'**a**·yin ra·'**ah** — literally, "evil eye;" having an *'ayin ra'ah* means "being stingy."

'**a**·yin to·**vah** — literally, "good eye;" having an *'ayin tovah* means "being generous."

Ben-HaM'·vo·**rakh** — son of the Blessed One (i.e., son of God).

Bir·**kat**-Ha·Mi·**nim** — blessing against the sectarians (probably the early Jewish Christians) added to the main synagogue liturgy around 90 C.E.

b'ra·**khah** — blessing, benediction.

77

b'rit-mi·**lah** (Ashk: bris-**mil**·lah) — covenant of circumcision; circumcision ceremony.

chal·**lah** — loaf or cake, and as such a special loaf of white flour bread made for *Shabbat*; but in Romans 11:16 it refers to the share of the dough set aside for the *cohanim* in accordance with Numbers 15:20 (where the word appears) and Mishna tractate Challah.

Cha·nu·**kah** (Ashk: **Cha**·nu·kah) — Jewish festival, the Feast of Dedication, celebrating the rededication of the Temple by the Maccabees in 164 B.C.E.; the first historical reference to it is in the New Testament, at Yochanan [John] 10:22.

co·ha·**nim,** sing. co·**hen** (Ashk: **co**·hen) — priests.

din-to·**rah,** pl. di·**nei**-to·**rah** — legal decision concerning the *Torah*.

drash or mi·**drash** (Ashk: **mid**·rash) — one of the four modes of rabbinic interpretation of a text: allegorical or homiletical application of it (literally, "searching").

E·retz-Yis·ra·**el** — the Land of Israel.

go·**yim** (Ashk. **goy**·im), sing. goy — nations, pagans, heathen, Gentiles.

Ha·G'vu·**rah** — the Power, the Majesty (i.e., God).

ha·la·**khah,** pl. ha·la·**khot** — (1) the system of statutes which is determinative in traditional Judaism (literally, "way of walking"), (2) a particular statute or legal decision. For more, see Chapter II, footnote 45. Adjective: "halakhic."

Kad·**dish** (Ashk. **Kad**·dish) — ancient prayer blessing God; resembles the Lord's Prayer; recited (1) in the synagogue to end a section of the service, (2) by mourners.

kal v'·**cho**·mer — argument *a fortiori*, signalled by the phrase, "how much more:" "If X is true, how much more so must Y be true!"

kash·**rut** — the Jewish system of dietary laws.

Ke·**fa** — Peter's name in Aramaic (it means "rock").

kip·**pah,** pl kip·**pot** — skullcap, yarmulke (Yiddish).

kol — all.

ko·sher (this is the Ashk. pronunciation, which is all but universal in America; the Israeli pronunciation is **kasher**) — fit [to be eaten, according to Jewish dietary law]. *Kashrut* is the noun meaning "the system of Jewish dietary laws." To "keep *kosher*" is to observe *kashrut*.

Ma·**shi**·ach — Messiah (literally, "anointed one"); translated into Greek as *Christos*, which comes over into English as "Christ." The expected king, foreseen by dozens of prophecies in the *Tanakh*, who would deliver the Jewish people from oppressors and bring peace to the world. The New Testament showed that Yeshua is this promised Messiah, and that his means for bringing peace included dying as the final sin-offering to atone for the sins of the world and rising from the dead to intercede for those who put their trust in him. At his second coming he will fulfill the national aspirations of the Jewish people and bring world peace.

Mat·tit·**ya**·hu — Matthew, a Jewish tax-collector for the Roman government who became one of the twelve emissaries (apostles) of Yeshua and wrote one of the four Gospels.

mi·**drash** (Ashk. **mid**·rash) — see *drash*.

mitz·**vah** (Ashk. **mitz**·vah), pl. mitz*vot* — commandment.

n'·ti·**lat**-ya·**da**·yim — ritual hand washing required before eating, according to *halakhah* (the Oral Torah), but not according to Scripture.

P'ru·**shim**, sing. Pa·**rush** — Pharisees, one of the two major religious parties in the time of Yeshua.

p'shat — one of the four modes of rabbinic interpretation of a text: its plain sense, what modern interpreters call grammatical-historical exegesis (literally, "simple").

Ram·**bam** — acronym for Rabbi Moshe ben Maimon, "Maimonides" (1135-1204), the best-known Jewish scholar of the Middle ages.

re·mez — one of the four modes of rabbinic interpretation of a text: peculiarities in the text are regarded as hinting at a deeper truth than that conveyed by its plain sense (literally, "hint").

San·he·**drin** — Jewish tribunal during the period of the Second Temple.

Shab·**bat** (Ashk. **Shab**·bos) — Sabbath, the seventh day of the week (Saturday).

Sha·**'ul** — Hebrew form of the name "Saul." In this book it refers to Saul of Tarsus, also known as Paul (see Acts 13:9).

Sha·vu·**'ot** (Ashk. Sha·**vu**·os) — Pentecost, one of the three Pilgrim Festivals.

Sh'khi·**nah** — the manifest glory of God.

Sod — one of the four modes of rabbinic interpretation of a text: using the numerical values of the Hebrew letters to reveal "secrets" that would otherwise not be noticed (literally, "secret").

Tal·**mud** (Ashk. **Tal**·mud) — Compilation of the Jewish Oral *Torah* made between the second and fifth centuries of the Common Era, comprised of the Mishna and the Gemara. The Soncino English version occupies about two feet of bookshelf space. Orthodox Judaism considers that the Oral Law (corresponding to what the New Testament calls the "tradition of the elders") was given by God to Moses on Mount Sinai along with the Pentateuch or Written *Torah*.

Ta·**nakh** — acronym made of the words *Torah* (Pentateuch), *Nevi'im* (Prophets), and *K'tuvim* (writings), which are the three main sections of the Hebrew Bible. Hence, the Old Testament.

tik·**kun**-ha·**'o**·**lam** — correcting, repairing, fixing the world.

To·**rah** (Ashk. **To**·rah) — Law (literally, "teaching").

treif — unfit to be eaten, according to Jewish dietary law (literally "torn").

tzi·tzi·**yot**, sing. tzi·**tzit** (Ashk. **tzi**·tzis) — fringes worn on corners of garments, fulfilling the command in Numbers 15:37-41.

Ya·'a·**kov** — James, Jacob. In this book the reference is to the brother of Yeshua the Messiah who became leader of the Jerusalem Messianic Community and who wrote the book of Ya'akov [James] in the New Testament.

Ye·**shu**·a — The Messiah's name, given him in obedience to Mattityahu [Matthew] 1:21. This name found some 30 times in the *Tanakh*, is a contraction of *Yehoshua* [Joshua]; it means "God saves" or "salvation." The name *Yeshua* was rendered in Greek as *Iēsous*, which in turn was brought over into English as "Jesus."

ye·shu·**'ah** — salvation, deliverance.

Yitz·**chak** — Isaac.

Yo·cha·**nan** — John, one of Yeshua's twelve emissaries (apostles), author of one of the four Gospels and of the three Letters of Yochanan [John]; it is also generally understood that he is the author of the book of Revelation.

Yom Kip·**pur** (Ashk. Yom **Kip**·pur) — Day of Atonement.

INDEX OF SCRIPTURE VERSES AND OTHER EARLY LITERATURE

TANAKH (OLD TESTAMENT)

NEW TESTAMENT

OTHER EARLY LITERATURE

GENERAL INDEX